roses

a comprehensive guide to care and cultivation

Amanda Beales

hamlyn

A Pyramid Paperback

An Hachette UK Company
www.hachette.co.uk

First published in Great Britain in 2006 by
Hamlyn, a division of Octopus Publishing Group Limited
Carmelite House, 50 Victoria Embankment
London EC4Y 0DZ
www.octopusbooks.co.uk
www.octopusbooksusa.com

This material was previously published as *ROSES*

Distributed in the US by Hachette Book Group
1290 Avenue of the Americas
4th and 5th Floors
New York, NY 10020

Distributed in Canada by Canadian Manda Group
664 Annette St.
Toronto, Ontario, Canada M6S 2C8

ISBN: 978-0-600-61467-8

A CIP catalogue record for this book is available
from the British Library

Printed and bound in China

10 9 8 7 6 5 4 3 2

Contents

Introduction

Roses are a fundamental part of my life and always have been, not only in work but also in leisure and, while I have no particular recollection of 'falling for roses', it is likely that I was influenced as a very young child by the passion my father bestowed on them. I am told that as a baby I would lie in my pram, guarded by the family dog, while my parents tended roses during the foundation years of my father's now world-famous rose nursery.

Roses have played a part in some key moments of my life. When christened at the tender age of just two months the vicar laid blooms of 'Zéphirine Drouhin', the well known thornless Bourbon rose, on the font. It was the only rose with blooms on in his garden (it was early winter), and while I may have been thornless then I am sure that the analogy was not quite so accurate when my father secretly had flowers of this and other roses flown in from Australia for my wedding day in late autumn! They made up a large part of my bouquet, which I recall had a heavenly scent and was probably delicious also, to judge from photographs of the horse pulling our wedding-day carriage. In turn, flowers of this beautiful rose were laid on the font at the christening of our daughter.

There are roses for every taste and nearly every possible situation, and flowers are available in very many colours, perfumes, shapes and sizes. Some are low growing; some have the capability of reaching the highest branches in the tallest of trees. Some flower for a long period, others for shorter times, and there are many with attractive hips and autumn foliage. There are roses that are in fashion and those that are relatively unknown. Throughout the plant directory in this book, I have tried to cover a good cross section of the many, many thousands of roses available, concentrating on an assortment of colours and habits, so that you, the reader, can appreciate the diversity of the rose and be guided as to the best ones for your garden. In the earlier pages I discuss all that you will need to know when growing them in your beds and borders, from preparing the soil to handling large, mature plants.

I love to indulge myself in the beauty and fragrance of roses; the naked garden of our newly acquired property is destined to be full of them, probably too full, for it is my intention to pack in as many different varieties as possible in as many ways as possible: mingling through the branches of trees, in hanging baskets and in more conventional plantings. I have a scheme in mind – lots of flowing, mingling colour and perfume with hips and interesting foliage. I have no doubt that I will continue to learn from my new garden companions and I look forward to the delights that are ahead.

Having worked in every aspect of rose growing, I have found that some of the most pleasurable times have been spent meeting fellow rose gardeners and learning to understand their common concerns and their desire to know more. I have drawn on this information and throughout this book have tried to respond to the needs of all rose gardeners, from those requiring just a little guidance in care and selection to others, like me, who are starting from scratch with a new or previously neglected plot.

I hope that while dipping into the text, or enjoying Mark Winwood's superb photographs, you will pick up on the romance of the rose and come to share in it with me; it is at the same time addictive, fulfilling and long lasting.

Amanda Beales

Right: Amanda has always had a passion for roses and is responsible for introducing numerous new varieties.

Using roses in the
garden

A lot has been written about the design of rose gardens and the use of roses in new, mixed schemes or in established gardens. I aim here to amalgamate some of these already recognized ideas and to encourage you to look beyond the obvious; there are probably places in the garden that you had never considered before as being good spots for roses.

Traditional supports for climbers and ramblers

There are many splendid ways of displaying climbers and ramblers on supports other than walls. Pillars and obelisks are two of the most obvious ones.

Usually around 2.5 m (8 ft) in height, pillars can be a useful way of training roses in the smaller garden, as little width is required. They can be made of any durable material. Rustic poles are probably the most economical but they can be much more formally structured,

Below: A structural feature is enhanced with roses beneath.

Above: Roses can be planted on one side of an arch and trained to grow over it, but if a less one-sided look is to be achieved they should be situated on both sides.

using lengths of 10 x 10 cm (4 x 4 in) timber, finished off with an elegant finial (available from good garden centres) and painted in any colour desired. Don't be afraid to experiment – the many different hues of roses allow for the adventurous use of colour in the garden. Wrought iron pillars and posts can also be purchased but they can be expensive; there are much cheaper galvanized steel versions that come quite close to the real thing.

When growing a rose on a pillar, whether it is a climber or a rambler, try to wind the stems around the structure rather than just tying them in vertically. Flowering stems are produced from the leaf joints and the more the branches are trained to the horizontal, the more flowers will be encouraged.

Obelisks can have any number of sides but taper off to a central point. As with pillars, they are available in all manner of materials and

styles. Simple, more rustic obelisks can be made from straight tree branches cut from hedgerows, but I would not endorse this on a large scale; long thick canes or lengths of thin timber are a better alternative. It is a good idea to plant the rose first, then place the branches or canes around it in the ground about 60 cm (24 in) apart, bringing them together at the top where they can be tied with raffia or string. The rose can then be trained around the outer edge of the obelisk as it grows or, if using a shrub rose, encouraged to stay within the structure with the intention that only the flowers appear on the outer edges, but this can be difficult to achieve.

Arches act as doorways in the garden, and if you have the space to create rooms or sections by planting long beds of climbing roses or other plants on either side of them this works really effectively in forming 'see-through walls'. There are several ways of doing this. One is to position pillars at equal distances apart in a line on either side of the arch and then place rope swags between the pillars; ramblers can be trained up and then along them to create garlands of flowers. If you prefer, the rope can be replaced by narrow sections of trellis. These are fixed between the tops of the pillars with another section lower down on which the roses can be trained, thus creating windows through the 'wall', or a series of arches can be positioned, giving a selection of routes through which to pass. To create a denser barrier, make the screen with full panels of trellis as the supporting structure for roses or other climbers, with the arched doorway positioned somewhere along its length.

If you do not have sufficient space, arches can be placed elsewhere, over a seat perhaps to create a bower, in front of doorways to sheds or other buildings, or over paths and gateways. Extra perspective can be created if a pathway leads to the arch, drawing the eye to it

Above: An archway or small pergola covered with roses frames the view to hidden gardens beyond.

and then beyond to some focal point, such as a statue, set further back. A mirror strategically placed beyond an archway can create the illusion of space in the smaller garden.

A pergola is a series of connected archways adorned with roses or other climbing plants forming a tunnel, under which one can walk. In truth, this is a feature ideally suited to larger gardens, although it may be possible to position one over a pathway in smaller spaces. Pergolas can be made from anything strong enough to take the weight of many heavy blooms. The roses can be planted in a regular pattern, with two of the same variety opposite one another forming bands of colour along the length of the tunnel or less formally with mixed varieties. The choice is either to go for a mass show of colour or to mix flowering times for a longer display but with less impact; either way, a cool shadowy tunnel will be the result.

When erecting a pergola, bear in mind that it should be wide enough for two people to walk through side by side, and that it should be at least 2.5 m (8 ft) tall to allow a few blooms to nod through unobtrusively.

The use of containers

Roses do not have to be grown in the ground, so why not try growing them in containers? The use of tubs and the like in the garden has two definite advantages. Firstly, it provides the scope to be more adventurous with shape and colour, and secondly, it makes roses portable so you can exchange one with another as the mood takes you.

There are all sorts of tubs and pots available to the gardener but there are also more original items that can be used for this purpose. A wheelbarrow, for example, that has outlived its practical use can provide the ideal container, and a large one would accommodate two or three smaller roses. Its life can be extended by including a polythene liner, but do ensure there is good drainage in the form of holes drilled in the bottom and a layer of pebbles below the

Below: Use dead tree stumps as containers; with a little manipulation they are natural in appearance and ideal containers when treated correctly.

compost. When the roses there have passed their best, simply wheel it to a less prominent position. Old tin buckets or even baths can also be used in this way.

To make a plastic pot more interesting, make a few holes around the sides and plant a few low, spreading bedding plants or moss in them, or paint it – bands of colour can be effective, as can sponge painting. There are also exterior textured paints available, but check on the label that they will coat plastic, it may be wise to rub a texture on to the pot with sandpaper first. If you have a particular rose in mind, choose a paint colour that will either complement or contrast with the flowers.

You could also plant an old pair of large gardening shoes, with laces and tongue, with miniature roses, underplanted with a couple of bedding plants; take the laces out and pull the tongues forward to make room for the planting. Again, add drainage holes to prevent waterlogging. Although they will not last forever, planters like these make an interesting feature on the doorstep and a conversation opener with callers.

Above: Rambling roses grown through the branches of trees provide high-level colour.

Roses in mixed beds and borders

Roses are excellent companions to other plants and can bring often overlooked qualities to the bed or border. They are chiefly sought for their flower form and fragrance, but do not forget that there are varieties that produce hips and autumn foliage, there are some with wonderful thorns and some best grown for their attractive leaves. Many shrub roses are interesting structurally as they mature and can be used as specimen plants in mixed borders.

If you have an unsightly tree stump in the garden, this too can be turned into a feature. Hollow it out, drill a few inconspicuous drainage holes through to the hollow and plant a rose in it. The procumbent, trailing type roses are effective used in this way. To extend the life of the wood, the sides can be lined with polythene. Eventually the base of the trunk will rot and the roots will find their way down to the ground below.

If you have a dead tree, consider planting ramblers so that they climb through the branches but make sure the tree is safe first. Ramblers can also be grown against live trees, but they will need plenty of water and food in their early years as the tree will use most of what is naturally available.

Trailing roses can be planted in large window boxes and miniatures in smaller ones. Hanging baskets also make useful containers and allow roses to be grown in a different way; again, the trailing varieties are best in these but they should be positioned where thorny arching stems do not catch passers by.

Right: The grey foliage of this companion plant is an excellent foil for the flowers of this rose.

Where roses predominate

A garden that features a large number of roses can benefit from companion planting.

Edging beds and borders with perennials such as lavender or catmint, or small shrubs like box that can be clipped to shape, finishes them off and prevents any low bare stems from

Above: Through this arch there is the immediate impact of flowers but the eye is drawn to the garden beyond.

showing. Include spring-flowering bulbs which, although not visible when the roses are flowering, will provide colour early in the year. Flowers of lilac and purple shades complement the majority of roses well, as do grey- and silver-leaved plants.

In recommending plants other than roses I am no expert, but the following are a few I like to see. The blue perennial salvias supply both contrasting colour and shape, as do delphiniums and foxgloves. Cornflowers and irises work well, although some irises flower before roses. Scabious, in particular my favourite 'Clive Greaves', are very elegant, and penstemons are found in many colours and are dense and low growing. Although not unlike roses in flower form, some of the peonies work very well, as do poppies and low-growing hardy geraniums. For grey foliage try one of the ballotas or artemisias, use stachys to cover the ground and deter weeds. Also look out for shrubs with purple foliage which lend themselves to the pastel shades of older roses, such as *Berberis thunbergii*. Buddlejas, in particular *B. davidii*, are quite large but will supply plumes of blue flowers, very attractive to butterflies, towards the back of a border.

Mahonias, although spring flowering, are evergreen and have attractive leaves, and hebes, even when not in flower, have dense evergreen growth. Clematis such as 'Jackmanii' and the blue wisterias can mingle with climbers and ramblers, and there are many perennials and shrubs with similar coloration that lend themselves to shrub and bush roses.

Think of the shape plants assume and try to combine a variety among roses. The tall spears of foxgloves and delphiniums contrast with the graceful presentation of shrub roses, and underplanting bush roses with bubbly annuals, such as gypsophila and pansies, provides another element and helps keep weeds down too. Think also of flower shape and size. There are very few roses with flowers smaller than 2.5 cm (1 in) in diameter, so masses of dainty flowers in clusters will contrast with the larger rose blooms. When borne in clusters, the flowers of the rose form heads of an umbrella-like shape (called umbels or corymbs) usually nodding over slightly; try combining these with cluster-flowering plants of a different form, perhaps with racemes or panicles of flowers, such as wisteria or Russian vine.

Nothing but roses

In a garden or border of roses alone there are two ways of approaching the design. The first is to go for as much year-round colour as possible, the second is to create a stunning *en masse* display for a shorter period. Both schemes have much merit. In my own garden, I want to enjoy roses for as long as possible, but as a visitor to a garden, at the right time, I am captivated by masses of once-flowering roses, which are stunning to look at and with an overwhelming perfume. We all admire daffodils and rhododendrons when in bloom and appreciate them all the more because their beauty is fleeting, so why not roses?

A practical answer could be a combination of both options. The short-lived beauty of the summer-flowering varieties will enhance the repeat-flowering roses when the garden is used most. The season of interest is extended using earlier and later flowering varieties, plus those with decorative hips and autumn foliage.

Using roses in garden design

Whether starting from scratch or adding a rose or two to an established garden, it is important to plan. Use books and rose catalogues to find the most suitable roses (the directory in this book should help) and have a few alternatives in mind. Impulse buying is not a good idea, as there is such a huge choice that the chances are you will pick something totally unsuitable.

If you want a whole new rose garden, proper planning is essential. It is all too easy to plant too many or too few and very difficult to remedy this once the roses are *in situ*. As a rough guide, I would suggest that shrub roses should be placed 1–1.2 m (3–4 ft) apart, bush roses at roughly 45 cm (18 in) and climbers at least 1.8 m (6 ft) apart. This is only an average, and with the climbers will give dense covering.

If you are mixing shrub roses, bear in mind their flowering time, combining summer, repeat and continuous flowering periods to avoid bare patches later in summer. Remember the other features of the rose: hips, autumn colouring, leaf colour and decorative thorns.

Rose hedges and boundaries

Roses can make excellent hedges and dense, thorny protective barriers. The Rugosas are the prime candidates, with an extremely thorny

disposition and strong, healthy foliage; many of them will produce big tomato-like hips after flowering and can be clipped with shears in spring to keep them in shape rather than pruning them individually. An assortment of species roses forms a truly delightful, naturally flowing boundary while the taller Floribunda roses will create a slimmer barrier.

Fences can be planted with rambling and climbing roses which, when trained out horizontally, will provide colour from top to bottom. If you live in the country, however, be prepared for deer and farm animals to nibble.

The wild garden

Species roses are a useful addition to a wild garden. To create a native garden use *Rosa canina*, the Dog Rose, or *R. arvensis*, the Field Rose, both commonly seen in hedgerows. *R. pimpinellifolia* and *R. eglanteria* with its apple-scented foliage are also natives. Roses attract many insects including bees and butterflies but they also lure greenfly and caterpillars.

Below: *Rosa arvensis*, also known as the Field rose, is a native of Europe and is often found growing wild in country hedgerows.

Selecting and purchasing roses

Whether you are buying one rose for a particular spot, or many for a new rose garden, I would recommend that you do your homework first. There are so many to choose from, all with different qualities. Set your priorities: is perfume the most import factor, or is it flower colour, or overall size and habit? Most specialist nurseries will have experts available to help you choose, but their task will be difficult if you have no preconceived idea of what you are looking for.

Bear in mind where you are going to position your rose or roses. There are situations that would be unsuitable for most roses: in shade or on a cool, shady wall for example. There is a section towards the end of the plant directory in this book which should aid in the selection of suitable varieties for such situations.

There are numerous books, such as this, on the subject of roses and a few encyclopaedias,

Above: Container roses are readily available during the summer months for instant purchases.

all valuable in aiding selection, but growers' catalogues are also hugely helpful and there are some interesting sites on the Internet. There can be no substitute, however, for seeing the roses in the flesh, to help with your decision. Descriptions of colour and perfume vary and conceptions of them differ; a rose considered scented by some may not be to others. There are many rose gardens to visit and it should not be too difficult to find your nearest one by asking at tourist information offices, or visit a rose nursery – even if they do not have a garden as such they will often let you look at the roses growing in the field.

Flower shows are another good way of seeing roses and you can take advice from the staff in attendance; even if you are not placing an order don't think that you are bothering them, that is why they are there. If the show is in early summer, such as the Chelsea Flower Show in London, the roses on display will have been forced under glass to achieve blooms and may be somewhat paler in colour than they should be, so check with the grower that they

Below: Pre-packed roses from outlets other than garden specialists are generally not good specimens. This one was purchased from a chain store in early summer, at least two months after it should have been taken off the shelf. It had dried out and there were tender young shoots struggling for lack of water and nutrition.

are a true representation. Also take into account the way in which they are displayed. Some growers will take the trouble to create as garden-like an exhibit as possible, with the various types of rose displayed in the way they grow. Others, however, will cut the blooms and arrange them in bowls and vases; the onlooker then has no idea of the character of their growth in the garden.

There are three main ways that roses are bought. Specialist growers dealing in mail order will despatch bare-rooted roses by post or carrier. Ordering can be done at any time, although the earlier an order is placed the better both for availability and ensuring an early position in the queue when the roses are sent. As they can only be dug up when they are dormant, roses will only be sent out at this time, usually between late autumn and early spring. While it is desirable, they do not have to be planted immediately, and can be left in their unopened package for a few days. If after this time it is still not possible to plant them, they should be heeled in. Most growers will also allow you to collect your roses on a pre-determined date so they can have them lifted and packed ready for you. If you are hoping to go along and purchase on the spot, it is wise to call the grower first. Plants cannot be manufactured to order so it may be that the variety you are looking for is sold out. Some growers will have a selection already dug, but if not it may take some time for your roses to be made ready. The names and addresses of specialist growers can be found in the classified sections of gardening magazines where they advertise on a regular basis.

Pre-packed roses can be found almost anywhere in winter and spring and often later than this, from supermarkets to department stores and on market stalls. Buying roses in this form is far from ideal. Packaging of polythene containing peat to keep roots moist

encourages early growth and is a breeding ground for disease. Coupled with this is the fact that they have probably been stored at too high a temperature and will easily be damaged by low night temperatures and frosts when planted. If you must buy a rose in this way, take a good look at it through the packet if you can. If there are young, yellowing leaf shoots and the roots or peat surrounding them appear to be dry, put it back on the shelf: this rose is unlikely to settle well in the garden. It is sometimes possible to obtain root-wrapped roses. These are a form of pre-packed rose with only the roots enclosed in polythene. They are preferable to those discussed above as it is possible to study them better to determine quality and health. Look closely at the stems of the plant: if they appear at all wrinkled it is likely that the plant has been allowed to dry out at some point, and this is not a good rose to buy.

Container roses are from the same crop as bare-rooted plants, but have been potted so that they can be bought and planted during the summer. They can be obtained from most

Below: When planting a container rose in the summer you must remember that it will need regular watering, especially in dry weather.

21

Above: Check that the rose you are buying has a good structure of strong branches.

specialist growers and garden centres but probably only on a cash-and-carry basis, as they are awkward and expensive to transport. A specialist would probably prefer to sell you a bare-rooted plant during the winter rather than one that has been in a pot since the previous year or one that has been recently potted. It is best to leave a container rose in its pot for a month if it has been purchased early in the summer, to allow the root system to develop. If it is removed from its pot too early, the compost will not have had a chance to settle and will fall away, taking with it delicate young fibrous roots. If buying from a garden centre, it is possible that the rose may have been there for some time. If you are able to remove the pot the root system can be examined. Fine strands of root showing through the compost and holding it together are ideal, but if there are many thicker roots spiralling themselves around the inner shell of the pot, it has become pot bound and it is inadvisable to buy it as it is unlikely to transplant easily.

Above: Try to avoid buying plants that show signs of disease on their leaves.

Choosing a good specimen

If roses are coming to you via the post or carrier, it will not be possible to choose your own plants, but reputable companies operating a mail-order service will have their reputation in mind and will grade the plants in the field to avoid dispatching poor quality examples. The same applies if you are collecting a pre-placed order, as the roses will have been dug and packaged before your arrival at the nursery. If when you unpack them you are dissatisfied with the quality of one or more, contact the supplier at once rather than planting the rose and hoping for the best. It may make up into an excellent plant after pruning, and most do, but your case will be stronger if you report your problem early on. Good nurseries guarantee their roses and will honour this by replacing failed roses, although you may have to wait until the following season before receiving the replacement if a suitable plant is unavailable or the original died at the wrong time of year.

Left: A good specimen will have a well-formed root system and several strong branches, unlike the plant in the lower pictures which is spindly by comparison.

A good bare-rooted plant will have well spread strong roots and at least three strong branches, although some rarer varieties, especially Teas and Chinas, may have fewer and this should be expected if they are your choice. It should arrive damp, having been well soaked before despatch, and stems should not appear wrinkled or damaged in any way.

Obviously it is impossible to look at the roots of a container rose other than to determine whether or not it is pot bound, but if it is growing well it can be assumed that all is well. As with the bare-rooted rose, there should be an even arrangement of at least three strong stems that are not damaged. Check that there are no signs of disease and that the compost is moist. Above all, ensure that the plant is labelled, as there is nothing more annoying than getting a plant home and realizing you've forgotten its name.

Above: When planting a bare-rooted rose it is a good idea to shake the roots when half the soil has been returned to the hole to ensure that there are no pockets of air left.

A year in the life of roses

So you've chosen your roses. The calendar of events following will give you some idea of what to expect from them and what you should do both with new and already established plants but, if you don't follow this exactly, do not be too concerned; very few gardeners do, but still get good results. The most important areas are all associated with young plants, if you get it right to begin with you are more than half the way to good roses. For precise details on all aspects of rose cultivation refer to the following chapters; this is merely a summary of events.

Midwinter

Bare-rooted roses are available now. If you haven't already ordered or received them (they have been leaving the growers since late autumn) order them now. Certain varieties will no longer be available but many are still obtainable. Bare-rooted roses can be planted until early spring so you still have time but growers send out orders in strict rotation, so act now or you will be last on the list.

Other than planting there is little else going on in midwinter, unless you were severely hit with a disease in the previous season, in which case a wash with a fungicide may be appropriate. Take advice from your local garden centre or grower as to which to use, but ensure that you wash both the rose and the surrounding soil and, if appropriate, any support on which roses are growing. Spores from wind-spread diseases can overwinter in the soil or on dead leaves close by to re-emerge the following year.

Late winter

Any winter activities can take place in late winter and this may be the last month to complete them successfully, as roses can begin to grow in early spring. The time for pruning is late winter and early spring, after the worst frosts are over. If you wish to transplant a rose from one part of the garden to another this really is the last opportunity; doing so in early spring is more risky, as the ground will be beginning to warm up and roots starting to grow. Roses that have been in pots and tubs for two years or more should have some of their compost removed and replaced with new.

Early spring

Finish pruning early in the month and top dress with proprietary rose food. This is the last opportunity for planting bare-rooted roses, before the weather warms up. As the leaves begin to show, start a spraying regime if you intend to use chemicals, and repeat this every 10–14 days.

Mid-spring

Mid- and late spring are probably the least busy times of the year as far as the growing of roses is concerned, as flowers are not yet developed and disease is at a minimum, although you should keep up a spraying or organic regime to prevent it taking control. As the weather warms up, start to water new roses regularly, especially if they are in pots.

Late spring

Ramblers and vigorous climbers should now be producing growth. Tie them against their supports in the direction you want them to

Below: Bare-rooted roses ready for the nurseryman to despatch to the customer.

Above: Spent rose blooms should be removed in order to encourage further production of blooms.

grow, as the wood will be soft and pliable at this stage and it will prevent them becoming used to growing in the wrong fashion. This will need to be repeated throughout the summer if you are to remain in control of rampant varieties. If you are trying your hand at breeding you can start now on roses under glass.

Early summer

Tasks in the garden are increasing in number and this is particularly true when it comes to roses, but the beautiful flowers and perfumes act as inspiration. Watering of new roses will need to be done frequently, unless it is a particularly wet summer. Flowers that have now gone over will need to be removed and extra care must be taken to keep pests and diseases at bay. It is now, as the more established roses are blooming, that you will notice proliferation and suckers may be emerging from under the soil – these should be removed as early as possible. Hybridizing can take place out of doors now, and in commercial rose growing

this is the time when budding often starts.
Cuttings can be taken now but they will need
more looking after than if you wait for early
autumn. Keep tying in climbers and ramblers.

Midsummer

Roses are still blooming well but many will be
going over. All varieties that flower repeatedly or
continuously should be dead-headed to
encourage the next flush, as should once-
flowering ones unless they set hips. Apply a
second application of rose food to support
growth into the autumn. Chemical or organic
pest and disease control should still be going
on, as should watering of young and potted
plants. Remove any recently developed
suckers and any leaves that have escaped
control and become diseased.

Late summer

Late summer can be a bad time for disease so
try to keep on top of it, both in precautionary
control and in the removal of diseased leaves.
Other than this there is little of excitement
happening. Keep up the watering and training
of climbers and ramblers, although their growth
will have slowed down now.

Early autumn

Many roses will have stopped producing large
numbers of blooms, perhaps an odd one here
or there, but a few will be blooming well at this
time. Remontant shrub roses can look quite
unkempt by now and will not mind a bit of a
tidy up, but leave the once-flowering varieties
or you will remove next year's flowering growth.
Keep up pest and disease control and
watering. Hips are now fully formed and some
roses will be showing signs of magnificent
autumn colour.

Left: Hips of Pimpinellifolia roses are always mahogany
brown in colour.

Above: A few varieties of rose suffer from viruses which are
not contagious to other roses but are often represented by
miscoloured leaves.

Mid-autumn

Roses are now beginning to slow down ready
for their dormant period. Cut down on watering
but continue controlling disease. Take
hardwood cuttings and think about
transplanting mature roses, but do not do this
until the plant is fully dormant. Rake up and
destroy fallen leaves, as they may harbour
unwanted disease spores. Prepare for any
bare-rooted roses you may have ordered, by
improving the soil and digging the holes.

Late autumn

Bare-rooted roses are now available. The
dormant season arrives at this time, and the
activity going on now can be done at any point
until early to mid-spring. Roses can be moved in
the garden if necessary and winter washes
applied to prevent spores of diseases such as
rust and blackspot overwintering. Protect
tender varieties to keep the frosts that are soon
likely to arrive from damaging or killing them.

Early winter

Early winter is as late autumn, except that the
risk of frost is increasing, so it is a good idea to
check that the protection you have put in place
for less hardy varieties is still secure.

Planting and pruning roses

Soil improvement

Giving a rose the right start in the garden is probably the most important thing you will ever do for it, which is why preparation and planting procedure are so important. Roses enjoy a slightly acid to neutral soil, one with a pH of about 6.5, but they will tolerate a degree of alkalinity and will not show signs of being unhappy in soils of up to a pH of 7.5. If you are in doubt as to the levels of acidity or alkalinity in your soil, testing kits are readily available from garden centres and are easy to use. As a rule of thumb (except for city dwellers), if there are Dog Roses growing in hedgerows nearby your soil is likely to be suitable for roses.

If you do find that your soil is too alkaline, it can be improved with the addition of some well-rotted farmyard manure; peat will do the same but it is a finite resource and should therefore be used sparingly. Garden compost is usually quite acidic but ensure that it is well rotted.

Even if your soil is not alkaline, it will still benefit from the addition of organic matter which will improve the structure of the soil as well as adding to its nutritional value. Organic matter will also help maintain moisture in free-draining soil as well as help improve heavy, water-retaining clay.

Conversely, if your garden is too acidic the addition of powdered lime will help. Much is said about the use of chemical fertilizers in the soil, but opinions constantly change, just as they do regarding human nutrition. Some believe that they reduce resistance to disease, in particular to rust, but I have yet to experiment. What is certain is that in an increasingly urban world, the freedom to obtain

Right: Soil can be improved with the addition of man-made or garden composts, well-rotted farmyard manure and fertilizers. It is wise to check the pH of the soil before using additives to keep the balance around neutral.

natural nutrients is decreasing and occasionally soils need a pick-me-up; if the use of chemical fertilizers is not overdone I cannot help but feel that they are appropriate. What is even more important is that plants receive a balanced diet of nutrients. We cannot be sure that this is the case when using organic matter, but the man-made alternatives are carefully mixed to ensure a balance.

Whatever the make-up of your soil, it will benefit from good old-fashioned double digging before it is planted. This may not be possible if you are adding roses to existing planted areas, but if you are starting from scratch it will both aerate the soil, making root penetration easier and bury surface weeds and weed seeds. To double dig an area, first remove a trench of soil a spit (spade depth) deep leaving it in the wheelbarrow or on a tarpaulin laid across the ground, and fork over the bottom of the trench. Then dig another trench adjacent to the first, returning the soil to the first trench, again forking the bottom of the new trench. Continue to do this until you have an empty, forked trench at the end and fill this with the soil taken from the first trench. If you do this in autumn but do not intend to plant until early the following year, you will be able to leave the clods of earth solid, as winter frosts will break them up and a fine tilth will be easier to create nearer planting time. If, however, you plan to plant close to the time of digging, it will be necessary to create a finer tilth at the same time.

If your soil is very heavy it may need additional drainage and this can be done at the same time as double digging. Roses hate being dry but will not thrive in waterlogged ground either. There are several ways of doing this. If you are planting in isolated positions, rather than a quantity of roses together in a bed or border, the easiest solution is to dig the hole to twice the necessary depth and lay some shingle in the base. For the rose bed or border, however, it is worth laying more sophisticated drainage in the form of plastic piping, although you could repeat the shingle application at regular intervals.

Specific replant disease

Roses should not be planted in places from which other roses have been recently removed, for the soil will be 'rose sick'. It is believed that roses leave certain chemical secretions in the soil which are offensive to other roses. The new ones will grow poorly, often suffering from die-back, and will often be very prone to disease.

There are a variety of ways of approaching this problem. The first is to plant the area with some other plants, thus giving the chemicals time to leach away, but this should be for a minimum of two years. The most obvious instant solution is to interchange the problem soil with some from another 'clean' area of the garden, but this is clearly not practical if you are replanting an entire bed or border; this is where the use of chemicals comes in. There are sterilants available that in certain dilution claim to rid the soil of rose sickness and by and large they are quite successful. You can not replant immediately but you do not have to wait too long. The alternative is to employ professionals to sterilize the soil using gas pumped under polythene but this is only economic on a large scale, for municipal plantings or other large gardens open to the public, and not necessary in the average house garden.

Rose sickness is the reason why commercial growers rotate their crop using different fields in separate years, leaving some dormant, or letting them to farmers who will crop them with something entirely different.

Above: When planting bare-rooted roses, the hole should be wide enough to accommodate the roots when spread out and deep enough to cover the base of all the stems.

Planting roses

The rose you are dealing with will either have bare roots or be in a pot. At the end of the day the results will be much the same, but since there are fundamental differences in the way they are planted, I will deal with each of them separately.

Planting bare-rooted roses

Before you plant a rose you need to identify the union. This is the gnarled area between the roots and the branches; it is the place where the rose was originally budded and you will probably be able to see where the top of the rootstock was cut off. The hole you dig should be deep enough that the union is about 2.5 cm (1 in) below soil level to deter suckers. Some of the older shrub and climbing roses may even develop their own roots from the area of stem below the ground. The hole should also be wider than the breadth of the plant's roots, when they are spread. This will ensure future stability because the roots will be encouraged to grow in all directions through less compacted earth.

Now you have dug your hole it is a good idea to break up the soil in its base a little with a fork, to assist root penetration, and mix a handful of bonemeal into it. Cast another handful of bonemeal over the soil that will be put back in the hole and mix this in as well.

Now position the rose in the hole, spreading the roots out and holding the plant upright. Add some of the soil so that it stands freely on its own, then return about half the soil. Shake the roots at this stage to avoid pockets of air being trapped and firm gently with a foot before returning the remainder of the soil. Once again, firm with the feet before tidying the surface soil and labelling if necessary. If planting took place

in late autumn or early winter, it is wise to check the stability of the rose plant a couple of times before it starts to grow in spring. No fibrous roots will have been produced to anchor it in position and the wind may have caused it to rock a little. Once it does start to grow it will require regular watering.

Planting containerized roses

To ensure that the compost is moist before planting, it is wise to soak the pot in a bucket of water, or similar-sized vessel. As with bare-rooted roses, the hole you dig should be wider than the pot and deep enough to cover the union. It is quite likely that the nurseryman will have left the union showing as rose roots are often difficult to fit in a pot (roses are not actually grown in pots but containerized at around 18 months old). Fork the base of the hole, mix in a handful of bonemeal and add another to the heap of soil waiting to be returned to the hole.

When removing the rose from its pot, try not to disturb the ball of compost surrounding the roots as this will cause the young fibrous roots to be broken. In the days of polythene pots this was easily achieved by slitting the polythene with a knife, but it is more difficult with a rigid pot. Don't grasp the base of the rose to pull it out as this too could disturb the roots. Instead, turn the pot upside down and tap its edge against the edge of a work-bench or table top. If it resists, squeeze around the sides of the pot gently and then have another go. Once it has been successfully removed, place it in the hole

Left: 1. Add stones to the base of the pot to aid drainage.
2. Ensure that the rose can be placed deep enough to cover the base of the stems; if it is too deep, add a little more compost to the bottom of the pot. **3.** Leave about an inch between the level of the compost and the edge of the pot, to prevent compost running away as the plant is watered.

and position so that it is upright; sometimes roses are not upright in their container because the size and nature of their roots dictated that they could not be. Carefully fill the gap around the root-ball with soil, firming gently.

Standard roses

It is very important that standard roses are well staked and that the stake is positioned before planting takes place. First, dig the hole so that, in the case of a bare-rooted standard, the roots can be well spread and the mark on the stem, showing its previous planting depth, is well below soil level to allow for settlement. A containerized standard should be planted in a hole that is deeper and broader than the pot, for the same reasons. As with other roses, lightly fork the soil at the base of the hole and mix in a handful of bonemeal, both in the hole and in the heap of soil. The stake, which should have been treated with wood preservative, can then be driven in to a depth of at least 45 cm (18 in). It should be off-centre and on the windward side, and should reach to just below the branches. To make it easy and less harmful to the rose when changing the stake in years to come, a piece of drainpipe can be positioned in the soil at this time and the stake inserted into this.

Position the standard against the stake and hold it there using one of the ties. Now start to in-fill and firm with the feet, or in the case of a containerized standard, if the hole is not much larger than the root-ball, with the handle of a garden tool to fit the gap between the root-ball and the side of the hole. The ties should be positioned at the top, bottom and centre of the stem, unless it is a half standard when two should be enough. Use spacers to prevent the roses coming into contact with the stake and loosely tighten. Remember to check them after about a month, as ground settlement may have caused them to move.

Above: This weeping standard is well supported with a strong, treated stake.

Moving established roses

Success in this endeavour will be determined by the age and size of the plant in question; a huge rambler will clearly be more problematic than a bush rose, and will have larger roots, making it difficult to dig up intact. You should only attempt to move roses in their dormant season, when they are not in leaf and will lose very little water.

First, cut back the branches fairly hard; don't worry too much about exact pruning at this stage, it can be done later when there will undoubtedly be some die-back to remove in any case. If the rose is isolated enough, dig a trench as deep as possible around it, for ease of movement when it comes to digging below the roots, which is the next task. If the rose is especially large, this can sometimes be a two-person job. As you dig, the plant should be gently pushed away from the side you are working on so as to give you easy access nearer the middle.

Once you have completed the removal, the rose can now be replanted in its new position, following the guidelines for other roses. Watering with a liquid seaweed extract before planting will encourage new root development. Don't forget that it will probably be very thirsty.

Planting a rose hedge

Rose hedges can be formal or informal. Informal hedges are best created from different varieties of roses combined for a natural mixture of flower colour, form and overall growth habit, and therefore should be planted with this in mind. Formal hedges of one variety or a mixture of similar roses, such as Rugosas, should be planted in a regimental fashion with the plants at an equal distance from each other. If a broad barrier is desired, two rows of the roses can be planted adjacent to each other but with the plants assuming a zig-zag pattern, so as to create depth and fullness between them.

To mulch or not to mulch

A mulch is a layer of material, either organic or non-organic, designed to retain moisture in the soil and suppress weeds. The effectiveness of it rather depends on the material chosen. Black plastic sheeting or the modern polypropylene version are probably the most successful of all, but do you really want them spoiling the appearance of the garden? I would only advocate their use if the roses are of procumbent nature, so that they will eventually hide the ugliness of the material. Used under such roses, this type of sheeting will suppress weeds until such time as it breaks up, which is useful as it is most awkward to weed through procumbent roses.

There are several other options when it comes to choosing a mulch. Bark chippings are quite good, but in time they will disintegrate, providing good organic matter but no mulch, or blow away. Cocoa shells are also a possibility and are fine so long as you can put up with a chocolate aroma pervading the garden. Some use grass cuttings, but they are very high in nitrogen and will encourage fewer flowers and much young growth, which will be more susceptible to disease.

Probably the most successful, unobtrusive mulch is shingle. In time weeds will get through but it will cool the soil and not blow away, and although in time weeds will get through, they are easily removed. There are several different types available but the choice will be dependent on personal taste and the style of the garden.

Below: A mulch can be made of compost or more refined bark or shingle.

Pruning and training

Why prune roses, you may ask. The answer is simple. It prevents plants from becoming top heavy, rejuvenates growth so that more flowers are created and helps eliminate disease by removing older growth that has previously suffered and may be harbouring overwintered disease spores. Pruning, coupled with training where necessary, also gives the gardener the chance to become a designer in some small way, especially with climbing, rambling and larger shrub roses; they will never be ideal subjects for topiary but they are controllable. Pruning a rose should not be seen as a sadistic procedure but should be viewed more like a hair-cut for the benefit of the plant.

Pruning is not the difficult assignment suggested by some although it can be time consuming if you have several roses, but also rewarding. You do not need many tools: a good sharp pair of secateurs, loppers for thick or high branches and a thick pair of gloves.

Above: Train climbers and ramblers in as many outward directions as possible to encourage lateral growth.

Scissors, especially those used by florists, are useful for daintier candidates such as miniature roses.

When pruning, always consider the following points. Wood that has become damaged in some way, by rubbing against other branches or being snapped in the wind, and swollen areas around old ties, should be removed as areas such as these provide ideal entry for disease. When two branches are touching but are not yet damaged, it is a good idea to remove one before they begin to chaff each other, and any diseased growth should also be cut away. Try, where possible, to make cuts at an angle, above and slanting away from a bud, and bear in mind which direction that bud is facing: you do not want new branches to grow towards the centre of the plant. Shrub and bush roses should be kept open, if possible, by removing central tangled growth and climbers should either be well tied in against their support or pruned with shape in mind.

Pruning newly introduced roses

Before looking at the methods employed in annual rose pruning, it is important to understand the necessity and benefit of hard

Below: Check ties to prevent them becoming too tight as the plant grows and branches thicken. The wire on this branch has caused damage that will attract infection.

pruning a newly purchased bare-rooted rose. Whatever the type of rose in question, its branches should be heavily reduced in size; bush or shrub roses to around 15 cm (6 in) in length, and climbers and ramblers to about 25 cm (10 in). If you do not do this, the outcome will be top-heavy plants with sparse and bare branches at the base. It is very difficult to encourage low growth later on in the plant's life, so at its first introduction to the garden, it must be dealt with harshly. I myself have fallen victim: it is so easy to give the desire of enjoying early and previously unknown flowers priority over the shape and performance of the plant. In several instances I have had to underplant with perennials to disguise the leggy results of my neglect.

Roses purchased in containers do not require any pruning until the correct season arrives, as the grower will have already given them the necessary treatment at potting time.

It is also worth checking the 'snag' at planting time. This is the area of the plant at which the branches of the understock were cut

Above: Light pruning during the growing season will encourage new flowering growth as well as keeping the plant tidy.

away from the roots once the implanted bud had been accepted in the process of commercial production. It is noticeable as a protrusion from the union (the area between the roots and branches) which looks like a branch that has previously been well pruned, in other words a stump. It should be reduced in size so that it is flush, if possible, with the union. If it is left protruding it is possible that it will, in turn, produce fresh branches of the understock which, as they are technically suckers, are likely to be more vigorous than the budded cultivar. In this scenario they will prove themselves stronger, depriving the upper part of the plant of nutrient and eventually taking over.

If you have purchased your bare-rooted rose direct from a reputable nursery, the snag will undoubtedly have been removed. Wholesale companies and, in turn, their outlets may be less concerned with such detail.

Ramblers

Rambling roses by and large flower on the growth they make in the preceding season and this is usually, although not always, in the form of long arching canes. These grow with much vigour from the base of the plant, although on occasion similar new growth will form higher

Below: A hard-pruned rambler will produce strong new growth from the base.

up. In their first year or two, assuming they were hard pruned on arrival if they were bare-rooted plants, it is best to give them their freedom to establish and form a good root system and begin to flower (ramblers will often take up to three years to produce blooms). Thereafter a pruning regime can be established. They should be pruned in late summer after flowering; it is foolish to allow the plants to expend nutrients on branches that have already flowered unless, of course, they bear hips, in which case pruning should be left until early spring. Canes can be trimmed to any length and will still be flower productive, but if they are all removed completely your rambler will be devoid of bloom.

There are two ways of pruning a rambler, entirely dependent on the manner in which you wish it to grow. When trained out horizontally, on a fence for example, the plant will withstand the removal of all growth that has previously flowered: the new canes can then be trained to form the overall structure. To achieve this you will need to remove the ties holding it in place, allowing it to fall away towards the ground. Work can then commence and once completed, or during pruning, the selected remaining growth can be re-attached. Encourage canes as they grow, with regular tying in, into a fan shape or outwards in both directions. This keeps the plant young and thin while encouraging new growth but is not always practical, especially if the purpose of growing the rambler is to disguise an eyesore. If you want a more permanent although deciduous disguise, be less severe in pruning, removing only the older wood, but still be hard on the odd branch or two to keep some young growth lower down.

Some ramblers are best left unpruned, especially those climbing through the branches of trees or sprawling on a bank; their position may make it impossible anyway. Most ramblers

will be happy if never pruned or if they are left unpruned for three or four years, especially the most vigorous tree climbers, but to encourage rejuvenation a good hard prune now and then will work wonders.

Climbers

Climbers flower on current season's growth and are therefore treated a little differently. They will send out strong climbing stems but these are usually slower growing than those of the ramblers. As young plants they should be trained outwards as much as possible and fixed to the trellis or the support you have in place. From these branches will grow the 'lateral' stems that produce the flowers. With age, climbing stems will appear higher up and these too should be spread outwards to encourage flowering. When pruning, reduce the lateral stems to about a third of their length and they will produce flowering stems the next summer, which are then treated in the same way, and so on in future years.

As with all roses, but most important of all with climbers, watch out for rubbing stems. Their growth and the training method employed for these roses is such that stems are very likely to come into contact. Rubbing stems will soon become chafed and such damaged areas will provide ideal conditions for disease to enter.

Once-flowering shrub roses

Included here are the Gallicas, Centifolias, Mosses, Albas and Damasks as well as the diverse species roses. Other than when growth is untidy, it is often best to leave these particular roses unpruned. If they need a trim it is best done in summer just after they have

Above: This shrub rose has become untidy and has many crossed stems which will start to rub against each other if some are not removed.

Below: The shape is now improved and the effect of the pruning will be that more growth is produced lower down on the branches that remain.

flowered, enabling them to make more flowering growth before the frosts, for the following year. Don't prune varieties that set hips unless you have to, as autumn hips are a great source of pleasure at a time when there is less interest in the garden.

If you do prune, concentrate on areas of weak and damaged wood, or leggy dense growth that may make the rose look top heavy. Above all, try not to spoil the character of the plant or be too harsh in your treatment; severe pruning is best done during the dormant season, when there will be less water loss, although it will reduce the flowering potential for that year.

Repeat-flowering shrub roses

Pruning roses from this group will benefit both their shape and flowering capabilities. Thin out the plant if it is becoming too dense, remove thin growth that is unlikely to produce or support heavy flowers and remove any damaged growth. When this is done, the main stems can be reduced to different levels, some by about one-third of their length, from which earlier flowers will appear and some by about two-thirds, from which new growth will be encouraged lower down and will be of benefit to the plant in future seasons. The following year, taller branches can be treated to a low prune and those cut hardest the previous year can be left taller, thereby creating a rotation of younger growth. Summer pruning can be done, if necessary, when dead-heading but this should be a light trim for the benefit of appearance rather than a full-scale prune. If you have a variety that produces hips, dead-head the early flowers but leave the later ones untouched, otherwise you will obviously loose the hips.

Above: Hybrid Teas and Floribundas should be hard pruned each year to prevent them becoming top heavy.

Pruning bush roses

Bush roses are candidates for hard pruning, especially in their first year. The principle is to keep growth low, as they quickly become leggy and top heavy if not dealt with regularly, and to maintain an open well-shaped plant. Thin, bendy stems are unlikely to produce good flowers, so these should be pruned the most, leaving the stronger branches to form the shape and character of the plant. Try to cut above an outward-facing bud to prevent overcrowding in the centre of the plant and remove any dead or diseased wood. When removing branches at their base, make the cut as low down as possible, as after several years of this treatment the plant will look most

unsightly if there are lots of dead stumps here. In the autumn, after flowering, trim bush roses back a little, both to tidy them and make them less prone to rocking in mighty winter winds.

Standard roses

Standard roses come in three forms, and are simply a bush, shrub or climbing/rambling rose budded on to a host stem; it therefore follows that the pruning and training principles are much the same as for that cultivar not grown as a standard, so I refer you back to earlier text. The exception to this is the weeping standard because the desired effect is for the branches to cascade down, not grow up against a support in the way ramblers and climbers are encouraged to. There are three ways of doing this. The first is to purchase a trainer: this is an umbrella-shaped wire frame, rather like an upturned hanging basket. This is attached to the top of the stake (which has to be taller than the standard stem) and fits over the branches. The theory is that the leaves and flowers will grow densely enough to disguise it, but it is visible for quite some time and, I think, positively ugly. The second method is to attach a wire hoop to two or three stakes surrounding the standard and to tie the branches to it, but again I find this unsightly, although the device can be removed once the branches are heavy enough to remain there on their own. The best method by far, in my opinion, is to draw the branches in, by securing them with a length of soft string with one end fastened to the stake. The string is largely hidden by the branches and the whole effect far less contrived.

Whichever method is employed, it is important to create a balance of branches cascading equally on all sides. It is usual for the

Below: To encourage the branches of a weeping standard to fall, tie them towards the stake. As the branches grow the string will be hidden.

standard to have been budded in three places equidistant around the stem to guarantee an even distribution of branches but, on occasion, the plant may have only received two buds, in which case more care must be taken during the process of training. While I would not advocate the purchase of a standard rose that has received only one bud, experienced rose gardeners will have no trouble in training such a plant given time.

When you are pruning or training a standard rose, check the ties that hold the stem to the stake, ensure that they are not perishing or too tight, but also look for signs that they might be chafing the stem, in which case they are too loose. A standard should be supported by at least two ties, in the case of a weeping standard three if there are fewer you need to add to them.

Hedges and procumbent roses

Because there are a lot of twiggy branches on a hedge or in a large bed of low-growing, procumbent roses they can be treated in a more general fashion, rather than by tackling one branch at a time. They will even respond to being trimmed with an electric or petrol-run hedge trimmer, but do be careful if lots of thorny pieces of stem start flying through the air; wear eye shields of some sort. Many rose hedges are of Rugosa roses, which have wonderful autumn foliage and hips, but if you desire a neat and tidy perimeter finish you will need to prune the plants so that they are narrower at the top than they are at the base. More vigorous growth will appear higher up on the plant and by the time they come into flower the width will be constant. Prune the hedge to the height of the shortest plant to get an even finish.

Dead-heading

Dead-heading is simply speeding up nature's process of dealing with dead flowers. When a flower goes over, it, along with the uppermost part of the stem (all that is above the first leaf joint), will die and fall to the ground, unless the variety sets hips.

There are two ways of dead-heading roses: one is tried and trusted and the other is relatively new and, for my part, untried. To carry out the first method, select a leaf joint below the dead flower that is facing outwards, and cut away everything above this joint. The bud, hidden under the leaf stalk, will then grow and produce flowers. The advantage of dead-heading in this way is that you can control the shape of the plant a little during the summer, as well as the winter. The new method does not carry with it this possibility as less growth is removed: it involves snapping off the flowerhead at the abscission layer, which is recognizable as a slight bulge on the stem usually at the first leaf joint. It is said that the more foliage a plant has the better its performance, and also that the rose will produce its next flush more quickly and with larger numbers of blooms. I shall be trying this method at the earliest opportunity.

Below: Clusters of flowers should be removed just above a lower leaf joint.

Suckers

Throughout the growing season, suckers may well appear from the roots. If the plant is commercially produced by budding, these fleshy stems will be from the rootstock and are therefore not of the budded cultivar that appears above the ground. If the plant has been there a while, or if it was produced from a cutting, in other words if it is on its own roots, then the sucker need not be removed as it is part of the cultivar. To know the difference can be difficult, but it is an old wives' tale that suckers have seven leaves on a leaflet and cultivated roses five. This applies to some, but not all modern bush roses; many shrub roses, ramblers and climbers have seven. If you know that the rose was originally budded, the best way to determine whether or not the stem is a sucker is to trace it back to its place of origin, removing some of the soil around it to see what you are doing. If it originates from the root or low on the union (the barked area between the

Above: When removing a sucker, try to trace it back to its origin and remove it carefully and cleanly.

branches and roots) it is a sucker and should be removed; if it comes from above this area it should be left. If you are still unsure, compare the leaves and thorns with similarly aged parts of the rose itself. Are the leaves the same shape and colour? How many thorns are there and how are they shaped? Is the growth of equal vigour? Try a second opinion.

Suckers should be removed as soon as they are noticed, before they sap too much energy from the rest of the rose. If left, they will be seen to be much more vigorous than the cultivated plant and will gradually dominate until they take over completely.

You should trace a sucker back to its point of origin, placing the thumb between it and the root and forcing it away by pushing down. The tear should be as clean as possible to prevent it from re-shooting. Rose gardeners in days gone by had an instrument designed specifically for this called a 'spud', a long-handled tool intended to sit over the base of the sucker, and when pressure was applied it simply tore it away. If the sucker is the same as the plant itself, you may be able to remove it with some root attached. You then have another plant for elsewhere in the garden or as a gift for a fellow gardener, this is discussed in more detail on page 50.

Below: Shoots that appear on the stem of a standard rose are suckers and should be removed as cleanly as possible.

Propagation

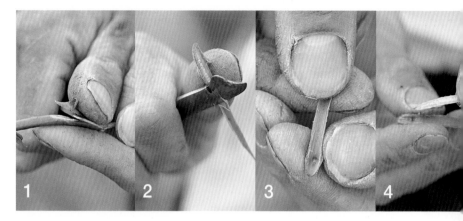

Above: 1. The scion is carefully sliced away from a stick of budwood. 2. The propagator trims the scion to the correct length. 3. The pith is removed from under the bark. 4. The tiny budding eye can be seen nestled in the cavity.

There are various ways of propagating roses; some require more skill than others but most can be done on a small scale in the garden with much success.

Budding

This is the method most commonly used by commercial rose growers as it uses small amounts of propagation material, has a high success rate and produces strong, saleable plants. The actual process calls for dexterity, and the novice will probably be all fingers and thumbs at first, but perseverance will result in the task being achieved successfully.

As budding is carried out at the peak growing season, during early and midsummer, it is necessary to act quickly to prevent the plant material from drying out. Commercial nurseries usually have a team of budders, but they will also often employ skilled propagators on a piecework basis who are capable of budding several thousand roses in one day.

Rose stocks are planted in the winter preceding budding. They are one-year-old seedlings usually of a species selected for good rooting qualities and vigour such as *Rosa laxa*, the most commonly used rootstock today.

A mechanical, tractor-drawn but manually operated planting machine is used to speed up the process of planting many thousands of the stocks in rows. Once planted, the soil on either side will be banked up around them to keep the area needed for budding moist and soft. They will then be left to settle and develop ready for budding to begin in the summer.

When the stocks and the propagation material from existing rose plants are ready, budding will start. First, the material needed will be cut from the previous crop. Lengths of stem, about 30 cm (12 in) long and roughly pencil thickness, which are mature but not old are cut from the plant. They then have their leaves removed, leaving only a piece of the leaf stalk. For ease of handling, the thorns are taken off. The stem is then ready for the budder and will be put, with other stems of the same variety, in a bucket of water until needed.

In the field, a tractor-operated brush will be used to expose the base of the stocks in readiness for the budder. Using a special knife, the budder will make a 'T'-shaped cut in the bark of the stock he is working on, opening it with the back of part of the blade or handle of the knife, taking care not to damage the flesh inside. He then cuts away the scion from the stick of bud wood complete with bark and leaf stalk, then removes the flesh from behind the bark to expose the bud. If there is no bud, it is discarded. The bud is then inserted into the cut on the stock so that the piece of leaf stalk is facing upwards. Any surplus bark above the bud is then cut away at the top of the 'T' cut and bandaged using a latex tie.

It soon becomes apparent if the bud has taken or not. If it has fused with the tissue of the rootstock it will begin to shoot, so the nurseryman will carry out a random check by removing some of the latex ties. If, for some reason, there is a large quantity of failures in a particular variety he may well re-bud the stocks using the side of the stock not already budded.

In the autumn, the bud will have developed into a shoot which is trimmed to encourage a bushy plant. Later, the top of the stock will be cut away, just above the site of budding, a process described as 'heading back'. There is now no possibility of competition for nutrients

Below: 5. The stock prepared for budding. **6.** A horizontal cut is made in the bark of the stock. **7.** A vertical cut is then made to form a 'T' shape. **8.** The scion is neatly slid into the bark via the cut. **9.** Once in position the top of the scion is trimmed away so that it is fully in place. **10.** A latex tie is secured over the newly inserted bud which will protect the site as the scion fuses with the stock. **11.** As the bud begins to grow the tie will perish and fall away.

between the newly added shoot and the branches of the rootstock. By the following summer there is a rose plant, called a maiden, which will be grown on in the field before it is dug in the autumn. It is likely that it will also supply the grower with bud wood for the next crop.

Budding a rose at home is identical in all respects to commercial budding except that it is done on a smaller scale. Most growers will be happy to supply you with a few rose stocks but you will have to find your own bud wood, perhaps from a plant you already have, or from a friend or neighbour who has a rose you admire but cannot purchase. Try to use a proper budding knife, but if you cannot get the latex ties used by the professionals, secure the bud with raffia instead, wrapping it around the top and bottom of the 'T' cut.

If you want to propagate a rose that is no longer obtainable but have no faith in your budding skills, speak to a rose grower. Most will be happy to bud a few plants for you at a charge similar to roses of the same type.

Grafting

This is another method used by commercial growers, usually to produce the few varieties that are not effectively budded. Once again it is the combining of a host root system with a scion, which together will eventually form one plant.

It is an operation that requires skill, learned through much practice, and the success rate will, by and large, be dependent on this skill. As in budding, the host plant will be chosen so that it influences the growth of the chosen variety, thus creating a successful plant. As with the stocks used for budding, the most common is *Rosa laxa*, usually produced from seed.

In midwinter, the nurseryman will place about 50 rootstocks in a bundle in damp but sterile peat under glass to stimulate early root activity. They will remain there for two or three weeks before grafting begins. At this time the bundle will be split and the stocks worked on individually. The top of the stock is removed about 5 cm (2 in) above the root and a downward cut made into the exposed tissue on one side. The scion will be of one-year-old growth, about 10 cm (4 in) long, and will have been cut on a slant at top and bottom. The bottom is given an inverted cut so that it matches the cut on the rootstock and they are then slid together, so that the smaller piece of rootstock is held inside the scion. The idea is to introduce the two exposed areas of cambium together, so that they fuse and become as one. Once this is done, the joint is held together with raffia or grafting tape and sealed with grafting wax to ensure that the wounds are kept watertight. The top of the scion is also sealed in this way to reduce transpiration.

The newly grafted plant is then splinted with a cane and potted, where it will remain, to begin with in a heated greenhouse, for the duration of the next year. During this time the tape or raffia will be removed to allow the plant to grow without strangulation. Once it is a year old it can be potted on or planted outside, depending on whether it is to be sold the following summer or lifted the following autumn as a bare-rooted plant. This method is the most commonly used grafting technique; there are others in which the types of cuts made differ from this, but in all cases the theory of fusing the scion and stock at exposed areas of cambium is the same.

Propagating roses from cuttings

Commercial rose growers rarely produce their stock from cuttings. Not only does this method of propagation require masses of material when compared to budding (a cutting is

equivalent to five or more buds), but the rose produced in this way will be slower growing and in many cases will not possess the strength of its budded counterpart. Having said this, there are many cases where growing a rose on its own roots is appropriate and, as not every gardener has access to the items needed to bud a rose, it may be the only way of reproducing a plant in the garden.

Hardwood cuttings are the best choice for roses. You should wait until autumn, when the wood has had time enough to ripen during the summer. To liken a cutting to a pencil may seem strange but in all possible cases the wood should be straight, and about the length and thickness of a pencil; do not make it any

Above: Cuttings can be placed in pots in the greenhouse or directly into garden soil outside.

shorter if you have a choice. The top should be cut at an angle, just above and away from a bud, and the bottom cut cleanly below a bud. There are two schools of thought about the bud at the base. Some suggest that it should be cleanly sliced away to expose more cambium (the layer from which the roots will be made), others see this as unnecessary. I have had success with both methods, tending to prefer the second, as a new shoot will form from the base bud. Whichever is chosen, the use of hormone rooting powder will speed up the production of roots.

Above: The layering process **1.** The branch is pegged into position in a shallow trench. **2.** The peg is firmed with the foot.

well, cover with a plastic bag and secure around the top of the pot with a rubber band. This creates the ideal environment to encourage rooting. Place the pot on a tray of well-watered shingle and ensure that this never dries out; the water will travel into the compost of the pot, preventing it from becoming too dry. By autumn, a good if small root system will have developed and the cutting can be moved on to a pot containing more nourishing compost, in which it can be hardened off during the following spring and summer. By the following autumn it will be large enough to assume its permanent position in the garden.

Dig a trench in a sheltered but unwater-logged area of the garden deep enough to take about half the length of the cutting. Put a little sharp sand in the base of the trench to stimulate rooting and place the cuttings in it at regular intervals. Infill with the removed soil, firm and water. If you do not have a suitable spot, put the cuttings in a pot with equal mixed quantities of soil and sand and keep in a cool greenhouse or cold frame. By early spring the next year, the cuttings will be making roots and beginning to become small plants. They should be left *in situ* until they become dormant in the autumn, when they can be transplanted to their permanent location.

Cuttings can also be made of softer wood during the summer but these will require more care. They should be shorter than hardwood cuttings, around 10 cm (4 in) is ideal, but should be cut in the same way below a bud at the base and above a bud at the top. Remove all foliage except the two top leaflets, which should be taken back to two leaves to reduce transpiration. Dip the bottom of the cuttings in hormone rooting powder and place them in a pot filled with an equal mixture of soil and sand, or a soil substitute such as perlite. Use a dibber to avoid damaging the delicate wood. Water

Layering

Layering can be an extremely effective and simple way in which to produce new plants in the garden, but is a propagation method suitable only for roses with long arching growth that can be stretched out to touch the ground, which is why it is an uncommon practice.

Choose wood that is roughly a year old and pull it away from the plant so that it touches the ground at around 30 cm (12 in) from the growing tip and mark this place on the soil. Allow the branch to spring back up and create a shallow trench at the place marked. Pull the branch back down and peg it into position in the trench with strong bent wire. You can, if you wish, wound the bark with a knife to stimulate rooting. Once you have filled in the trench it is simply a case of waiting for roots to form.

Layering is best done in spring, when growth activity is at its peak and you will have a good idea if rooting has taken place when the protruding tip begins to grow. Check by carefully brushing away some of the soil at the place of pegging. Once roots are established, the parent plant can be detached and the new rose transplanted to a more suitable position, or potted on in the following dormant season.

Above: A newly germinated rose seedling.

Division

The method of dividing plants for propagation purposes is commonplace with perennial plants and virtually unheard of with roses. This is because the vast majority of roses are grown on host roots, so any shoots from the ground will be suckers of the rootstock, not of the variety that is apparent above ground level. However, roses that have been grown from seed and varieties growing on their own roots are candidates for this method of increasing roses.

It is not uncommon to find suckers of the old Scotch Briar roses, Albas, Rugosas and some of the other old roses growing in unexpected situations in old gardens. They are probably nowhere near the site of the original plant, which had long since lost all vigour and disappeared. Provided they can be lifted with some root intact, they can be moved to other areas of the garden during the dormant season or potted as gifts for other gardeners.

Micropropagation

This method of propagating roses is likely to be more and more prevalent in the future, but it is unlikely that the gardener or nurseryman will ever be involved since micropropagation is a form of tissue culture and, as such, requires sterile laboratory conditions. It involves the production of plants from cells extracted from the growing tips of the rose. These are stimulated to produce more and more growing points until a small plant is formed. Roots are encouraged with the use of hormone agents. Once large enough to handle, the rose is gradually taken off the man-made fibres and encouraged to grow in horticultural composts.

It may well be some time before the practice of micropropagation is commonplace because there are many types of roses that grow less well on their own roots than they do if they are budded or grafted, but there is undoubtedly a place for it. Who knows, one day all plants may be produced in this way and future generations of rose growers may have to have scientific training of some kind.

Growing roses from seed

Most garden roses will not come true to type if propagated from seed but many of the species roses will. Of course, if they have been fertilized by bees or insects carrying pollen the result will

Below: Young seedling roses ready for growing on.

Above: Breeding roses **1.** The petals of the female flower are stripped away. **2.** The stamens are removed using a pair of manicure scissors or a knife.

be a hybrid, and although probably not dissimilar to the parent it may display some different characteristics. To prevent this, it is wise to isolate the plant or at least the flower. If the plant is in a pot it should be moved as far away as possible from other roses in the garden; otherwise, one or two flowers should be covered with paper cones to prevent outside interference until the blooms have gone over. Rose breeders work under glass or in tunnels to speed up the ripening of hips and extend their working season, but as this sort of control is not possible outdoors it is likely that only early blooms will provide viable seeds.

Once ripe, the seed pods or hips should be gathered in early autumn and the seeds extracted. The hip may contain any number of seeds. They should be kept, in labelled bags, for six weeks at room temperature and for another six weeks in much cooler temperatures of 1–3°C (34–37°F), often the temperature found in the lower part of a household refrigerator.

After this period of stratification, they are ready for sowing. Mix equal quantities of sand with garden compost; the gritty consistency of the sand helps break down the seed coat. Do not plant any deeper than 1 cm (½ in) below the surface of the compost. If you have heated greenhouse benches, they will speed up germination if set to 12–16° C (54–60° F). Germination ceases altogether at around 28° C (82° F).

Seedlings emerge with two rounded leaves which are almost succulent in appearance. It is best to wait until true leaves have appeared before potting them on. Transplant into small pots or plugs to prevent them being overwatered, and where possible, use a soil-based compost, growing the seedlings on in pots throughout the following summer. After this they can be potted on further or given a permanent position in the garden.

Professional growers rarely grow roses from seed, as it is time consuming and the results are too variable. The only time this is not so is when breeding new varieties and producing rose stocks. Rose stocks are developed like this as it reduces the possibility of viral infection.

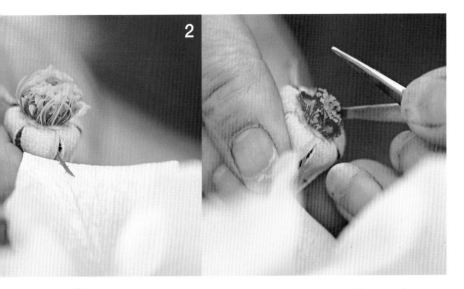

Breeding roses

All rose nurseries introduce new roses on a regular basis, whether bred by themselves or by an independent breeder. They do so for two reasons above all: the first is to fulfil the demand of the gardening public for ever better roses – although each and every one of us has preconceived ideas as to perfection, they can at least concentrate on major areas such as perfume and disease resistance; the second is for publicity purposes, as a new rose named after a famous celebrity or charity to which they are donating profits is far more likely to attract the attention of the public than the others in their catalogue and they will be remembered for having introduced that rose. Coupled with this is the fact that new roses are usually shown to the public for the first time at flower shows, where many other rose growers are also exhibiting. As in everything, there is much friendly competition between growers all hoping to gain media coverage of a new rose introduction at a show which, in turn, will bring in custom.

The hybridizing of roses is a complex subject and it is very easy to get bogged down in the botanical logic of genetics that dictates its success. It is possible to obtain excellent results with only a little knowledge and this is perhaps the best way to approach the subject. One can spend hours researching chromosomes and family trees when, frankly, it is just as well get on with the practical aspect of the work, as many of the resulting seedlings will be a disappointment regardless of the time spent working out which are compatible parents. As a busy person, this is how I approach the subject. I use the knowledge I have of the idiosyncrasies of individual roses, coupled with my appreciation of their beauty, when choosing which two should be put together. After a while, you get to know which make good parents, which set hips well, which encourage early germination and so on.

Most professional breeders will have a tunnel or greenhouse in which they house plants for the purpose of breeding. It is best to keep them under such cover as the rose hip, from which the seed is extracted, takes some time to ripen before the seed is viable. By

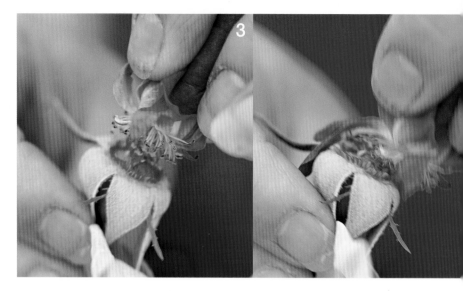

3

Above: 3. Pollen from the male flower is applied to the prepared flower either directly, as in the photograph, or with the use of a brush **4.** A label is attached to record the cross.

housing the plants in warm conditions you are able to start work earlier in the year and the hips will also be encouraged to ripen more quickly. It is also easier to control pests and diseases in a confined area, although the heat and often poor air circulation found in these places often encourage such plagues, so care has to be taken to deter them thoroughly. The roses will usually be grown in soil-based compost in large pots, but sometimes they will be planted directly into the ground. Where there are rose plants growing into the soil there may be problems with overwintering pests and diseases and, of course, they cannot be easily replaced with another variety because of replant disease.

The roses to be used for breeding should at all times be kept well watered and fed, with a high-potash feed. A rose that is struggling will not produce good quantities of flowers and will, subsequently, struggle to set hips. It will also be more prone to disease which, in turn, may affect the ability of the plant to produce hips.

Pests and diseases should be carefully monitored and dealt with, and a regular regime of control should be adopted even before there is any apparent sign of them.

One of the most common pests in the greenhouse or tunnel is the red spider mite which will move in, often unnoticed, in midsummer and then thrive in the dry still conditions, constructing delicate webs on hips and leaves. In a severe attack this particularly troublesome pest will cause the loss of some or all hips. Refer to page 64 for suggestions on ways to control it.

Roses for breeding should be placed in the tunnel or greenhouse in the spring, to encourage early flowering. If the plants to be worked on are in the garden this is clearly not possible, but it may be possible to erect a polythene structure over them to force them on, as the earlier that pollination can take place the sooner the hip, will be ripe. Good husbandry is important from the beginning to encourage blooms, so feed at this time.

Once flowers begin to emerge, the pollination process can begin. The selected blooms on the female or mother parent (that

which will produce the hips) should be between the stages of bud and open flower, when insects will have been unable to penetrate and pollinate the flower, thereby upsetting the planned cross. The petals should be removed, usually by grasping them and tearing them off all at once. If the odd petal remains this too should be removed, as it is the colouring of the petal that attracts insects in the first place.

It is now necessary to emasculate the plant to prevent self-pollination. Do this by cutting off all the anthers; a small pair of manicure scissors is ideal. Be diligent in this task, for just a few remaining anthers could spoil your work. The prepared flowers should be left in this state until the following day, when the stigma will have become sticky in preparation for the arrival of the pollen. This sticky secretion will cause the pollen to adhere to the stigma and will assist in the forming of a pollen tube, which will pass through the stigma and enter the ovaries, hidden in the receptacle.

After 24 hours the female parent should be pollinated. The pollen needed is often seen as a fine dust on the inner petals of roses, but if you are unsure as to whether the pollen on your chosen male parent is ready, gently touch the anthers with your fingers: ripe pollen will come away on them. There are two ways in which the pollen can be transferred to the female parent. One is to collect the pollen, placing it in an airtight container in which the pollen will last for 24 hours or longer given low temperatures, and applying it with a brush so that the stigma is visibly covered. Breeders who pollinate on a large scale will often collect the unripe anthers as they emasculate and keep them in a container until the pollen bursts from them, usually within 48 hours. The second way of transferring the pollen is to select a flower with ripe pollen, fold the petals back so that the anthers are foremost and brush these against the stigma of the female parent. The latter is an efficient method only if there are large enough numbers of desirable roses available to guarantee pollen availability and, as I am lucky enough to have large numbers of roses at my disposal, this is the method I tend to favour. It reduces the task to two stages with no need to worry about the care of stored pollen, and eliminates the necessity of keeping a number of cleaned brushes on hand.

Propagation

55

Once the pollen has been applied to the extent that you can see a dusty covering on the stigma, a label should be attached. I find it best to indicate both parents on the label with the female name first. If you follow the discipline of always placing this variety first on the label you will begin to gather together much valuable information for future reference. You will be able to determine the qualities of one parent against another as your experience increases and you gather personal knowledge and research in your own work, assuming you are serious; there are many commercially available but amateur-bred roses.

Once labelled, it is a waiting game. Some hips may not develop but there are different reasons for this. It may be that the two roses were not compatible for reasons such as their individual chromosome counts. Disease, lack of water, poor nutrition, too little pollen, bad weather and pests are all possible causes, any one of which may cause an isolated plant to suffer. Therefore do not expect perfect results, it is all part of the challenge. By early autumn, after about 16 weeks, the hips will be seen to be ripe and are ready for harvesting. There may be some hips that have not yet developed their autumn colouring, but nevertheless, if they are plump and fleshy they are still worth harvesting.

Collect the hips with labels firmly attached and take them indoors, or to a comfortable location, where the seed may be extracted; if there are many this is a time-consuming task. Carefully cut through the outer flesh of the hip so that you may pull it apart in two halves. The seeds will then be visible. Numbering from one to 30 or more, they are the hard, usually rounded kernels found within the fleshy pith. Use a knife to evacuate them into a container and wash them under the tap with the aid of a sieve. They should now be transferred into sealable polythene bags or other suitable sealable containers with damp sand or a damp

soil substitute such as vermiculite. The abrasive nature of these will help break down the seed coat (a layer on the outer shell which breaks down according to various natural factors such as frost, thus allowing germination of seeds separately over a long term to protect the species, in nature's way) through which the seedling plant will break out.

The seeds should be stored for about six weeks at room temperature and then for the following six weeks at a temperature of $1-3^{\circ}$ C ($34-37^{\circ}$ F), often found in the lower part of the household refrigerator. After this period of storage the seeds are ready for sowing. I sow seeds in trays with individual cells, which allow the roots to become established to some extent before transplanting, but seed trays are also recommended, provided that transplantation takes place before rooting invades the space of another seed, thus upsetting its chances of survival.

The initial leaves of the rose seedling, the first to be seen, are in a pair, fleshy and almost succulent in appearance. They will remain for a day or two before more characteristic leaves begin to appear. Once there are one or two sets of true leaves present, the plant can be moved into a small pot. Do not use any container bigger than needed in order to save time later on, as you will be tempted to water to the compost's capacity, which will be too much for the rose seedling.

As the seedling grows, it will begin to display its future characteristics in leaf form and colour. If you have been lucky enough to develop a rose with repeat- or continuous-flowering capabilities, it is likely to produce a bloom in its first year of life; although this will be smaller than the true bloom, it usually correctly shows colour, form and sometimes scent.

The new rose will need to be grown on in its pot and hardened off outdoors until it is large enough to provide propagation material. The

best way to increase its numbers is by budding, as it will then assume the characteristics it will portray should it be good enough for commercial production, but if these facilities are unavailable, a few successfully rooted cuttings will cover the possibility of the loss of the original seedling plant. The resulting roses should then be grown on under trial to ascertain whether or not the seedling possesses enough good qualities for introduction to the marketplace.

Commercially, new seedlings are included in the general propagation carried out by nurserymen and then planted in a trial bed, where they will remain for several years prior to possible introduction so that the description of the rose in the grower's catalogue is accurate. Once it is decided that the rose is suitable for introduction, it will be budded in large numbers over a two- or three-year period to build up enough stock of it and it will be registered with the necessary bodies, in particular the American Rose Society, under a trade name.

Above: Hips are left to ripen ready for harvesting.

A suitable name will be chosen for the rose a year or two preceding its introduction, either one that has been chosen by the grower or a name which has been requested by a charity body or private individual.

On a smaller scale, the amateur will need to approach a grower to introduce a new rose for them. The grower will still have to propagate it in order to build up enough stock, and will want to put it on trial it for a period to ensure that it has standards applicable to the status of the grower. They may also want to be responsible for the naming of it, but this would be done in consultation with the breeder. Roses bred by an individual but introduced by a grower should also be registered under a trade name.

If you wish to breed new roses for your own pleasure only, this is a delightful and rewarding pastime. The plants can be given a name chosen by yourself and make delightful, unique gifts for family and friends.

57

Pests, diseases and other rose ailments

Problems associated with roses are often the first reason gardeners give for not growing them, but this should not be the case. Rarely is a rose so susceptible to a disease or heavy infestation of pests that it is spoiled, and if it does get a little blackspot or mildew is it really that important? Nearly all plants are prone to one thing or another and we must not allow such problems to spoil our appreciation of them. Having said this, there are occasions when pests and diseases can get out of control and in these instances it is hard to ignore them, nor indeed should you, for the results can sometimes be devastating.

Prevention is always better than cure; the use of chemicals in the garden is a controversial issue and, where there is a choice, I prefer to be as organic as possible. There are some chemicals available for use in the treatment of roses that are kinder than others, not killing friendly insects, for example, and these are as good as their more cruel counterparts. Remember, however, that roses can develop a resistance to a particular substance so it is wise to alternate types used.

If you do choose to spray your roses in order to control their susceptibility, a regular regime is important. There is absolutely no point in an occasional blitz, especially when dealing with disease, as most fungicides are systemic (working from within the plant) and will lose their strength after a couple of weeks. Many insecticides, however, work on contact so if insects are the only problem you can treat only when they are present. There are chemicals available that will deal with pests and diseases at the same time, working just as well as two independent sprays.

If you cannot bear the thought of using chemicals in the garden you must select healthy varieties to begin with and look after them well. A well-fed and tended rose is much less likely to fall prey to disease than a neglected one.

As well as chemical insecticides, there are organic pest-control sprays available. They work by coating the pest in a fatty acid and are obviously a lot more environmentally friendly.

Diseases

Black spot

Black spot must be the best known disease of roses and there are varieties, as well as areas of the country, that are more prone than others. City centre dwellers may have less of a problem than those living in the countryside, as pollution tends to keep it at bay. The black spot spore is airborne and will settle on leaves where it causes a black or dark-coloured mark to form. These soon spread across the whole leaf, eventually causing it to fall. and on to younger stems, which become mottled and may wither. The disease can also be spread by using garden implements, such as secateurs.

The only effective control is to use a fungicide on a regular basis, at least once every

Below: Black spot first appears as small dark blemishes on the leaf which quickly multiply.

other week, from early in the season when the roses have begun to produce leaves and certainly before signs of the disease are apparent. Always follow the instructions carefully when using chemicals, for both safety and effective use. There are other measures that will help prevent re-infection. Always clear away any diseased leaves that have fallen to the ground, as they will be covered in the tiny spores that have the potential to overwinter ready to infect the following season. A badly affected plant can be washed with Jeyes fluid during the dormant season and it is also wise to wash any supports the rose may be against, as these can harbour the disease.

Above: Mildew often appears around flower buds.

Mildew

There are two forms of mildew found on roses. The most common is powdery mildew, and can be found on roses from fairly early in the season. It shows itself as powdery grey to white patches on young shoots and leaves, causes them to curl and prevents their growth. If it is not dealt with quickly, the whole plant can become affected.

A plant suffering from mildew not only has distorted growth but is far more prone to other diseases, such as rust and black spot. There are contact and systemic sprays available, and if a plant is known to be a sufferer they should be used well before there are any signs of it.

Mildew likes dry, still locations and will spread extremely rapidly in such situations, therefore try only to plant resistant varieties against walls or in very sheltered places. A regular wash down from the hose, both morning and evening, and keeping the plant well watered may help keep mildew at bay, but if you intend to be totally organic take advice on the most healthy varieties before planting roses in the garden.

Downy mildew can be a problem on roses growing under glass, caused by the extremes of day and night-time temperatures coupled with poor ventilation. It is unlikely to appear on roses growing in the garden. Patches of brown or bluish grey appear on mature leaves, causing them to fall, and on occasion these will also spread to the stems. The only effective control is to use fungicide, but if the problem is not great the infected leaves should simply be removed and destroyed.

Rust

Rust, probably the most harmful of all rose diseases, can often creep into the garden unnoticed as the small bright orange pustules attach themselves to the less visible undersides of leaves. Here they will multiply rapidly, spreading all over the plant and sometimes even on to the stems. As they mature they change colour through brown to black and will kill the leaf that supports them, causing it to fall to the ground. If the infection is bad the results can be heart-breaking: the rose will lose all its leaves and could die.

Action must be taken as soon as the rust is noticed. First remove all infected leaves and

61

destroy them. Then spray, either with a general purpose rose fungicide or a chemical that is more specific; a look along the shelves of your retailer will show you which to go for. Ensure that no fallen infected leaves are left, and gather and destroy them as well. A winter wash with a sterilizing chemical to cover the rose, the surrounding soil and any supports the rose is dependant on may help get rid of overwintering spores. If you have plants that suffer badly from rust year after year, it would be best to remove them from the garden as they will be causing the disease to spread to varieties that are not usually affected.

Above: Aphids collect on soft young growth and flower buds.

Stem canker

Stem canker is most often found on older plants, especially those that have developed much older wood. It is also seen on younger plants that have had the benefit of regular pruning over the years, where such wounds have allowed the entry of the disease. It may seem strange that I advocate regular pruning

Below: Caterpillars eat away portions of leaves.

but now report a drawback to doing so, but canker is easily dealt with and an uncommon enough phenomenon that it should not deter the gardener from pruning. Stem canker manifests itself in the form of large gnarled lesions, usually irregular in shape with shallow edges, swelling towards the centre and often with lifting areas of bark. The only available treatment is their removal. If in an awkward, structurally important place the lesion should be cleanly removed with a knife to expose

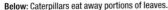

uninfected tissue and the wound then dressed with grafting wax so that it may heal, although in an older plant this may not work. If the canker appears on an area of stem that can be easily removed without detriment to the plant, then this is the obvious solution. Total avoidance of stem canker is impossible, but keeping wounds clean by using sharp implements when pruning will help.

Pests

Aphids

Aphids must rank as the biggest pest nuisance in the world of roses. They come in a variety of colours but the most persistent are greenfly, which love to gather and feed in large numbers on young shoots and flower buds. It is the sticky secretion, named honeydew, left behind that is perhaps the most annoying aspect of them as it is not only unsightly but coats the affected areas of the plant, covering breathing pores and therefore restricting natural growth. In bad cases, the honeydew may develop sooty mould which is black in colour and most unsightly. In days gone by, gardeners would purchase special brushes to remove the aphids or would spray them with soapy water, a method of control which is still considered worth trying today.

Until recently the only sure way of getting rid of these pests was with insecticide, but there are now organic sprays containing fatty acids which seem to do a good job. The most efficient natural predator is the ladybird and many garden birds enjoy picking them off as well, but they will never get rid of them completely, especially in a bad attack.

Capsid bugs

Less common than aphids, these annoying insects enjoy dining on the young growing shoots and leaves of roses. The effect is that

Above: Cuckoo spit is a protective substance housing the nymph of the frog hopper.

the growth becomes stunted and is left full of tiny holes. The only method of control is to use a systemic insecticide, but as the bugs move around swiftly from one plant to another they may be difficult to eradicate.

Caterpillars

Caterpillars do not seem to have a very fussy diet, seeming to enjoy any greenery in the garden and this includes the leaves of roses. Whole sections of leaf may be seen to have disappeared, almost overnight. There are chemicals available to control infestations but often search of the plant for the offender followed by its disposal may be the best and cheapest solution.

Cuckoo spit

It is not unusual to find a spittle-like foamy substance nestled in the leaf joints of roses. It is perhaps not a delight to the eye, but is insignificant in itself as it is actually the home of the frog-hopper nymph which is relatively harmless. If it is considered too unsightly, the best method of removal is to give it a sudden blast from the garden hose; otherwise, given time it will disappear.

63

Above: Red spider mites love hot airless conditions and are most troublesome under glass.

Red spider mite

This little pest can cause many problems under glass and occasionally, during the hottest of summers, on plants in the garden that are in very sheltered situations. Red spider mites love to be active in very dry and airless conditions, which is why they are most prolific from midsummer onwards. Invisible to all but the most scrutinizing eye, they will often have been present for a while before evidence is found in the form of very fine webs between leaflets and around buds. They live hidden on the undersides of the leaves, which is another reason for their apparent invisible arrival. They will often cause the egg-laden leaves to become dusty and limp before falling to the ground, where the eggs will then overwinter and hatch the following year. Eggs will also lie dormant in the fabric of greenhouses and tunnels, only to re-emerge there the following year.

Control is difficult and there is only one really effective chemical, Pirimiphos-methyl, but the new organic sprays also claim to rid roses of spider mite. I have not yet experimented with these and so have no evidence as to their effectiveness – suffice it to say that they are worth trying.

Sawfly

There are at least three types of sawfly that enjoy roses but two are the most damaging.

Leaf-rolling sawfly has the potential to completely distort all the leaves on an individual plant. The adult female lays her eggs on the leaf, while at the same time injecting them with a chemical that makes them curl up for the protection of her offspring. Control is difficult, for the damage will have been done before visible signs emerge. Spraying regimes with systemic fungicide in the early summer may help but the only other solution is to wait for leaves to fall, or to remove them, when they will be replaced by fresh growth. There is no great harm done to the plant, although it may be weakened and perhaps a little more prone to disease.

The slug sawfly is a little easier to control. It likes eating rose leaves, enjoying the fleshy parts but leaving the veins to form a skeleton leaf, a weird sight when it has devoured many leaves on one plant. Although less common than the leaf-rolling sawfly, its treatment is the same and usually more successful.

Thrips

Thrips love the tight full buds of some types of rose and will disfigure them by nibbling around the edges of petals. The damage they cause is cosmetic and by no means a deterrent to growth. As thrips tend to appear only spasmodically, usually during thundery weather, it is as well just to put up with them. If, however, they are proving such a nuisance that you cannot overlook them, you will need to spray the early opening buds with insecticide.

Animal pests

If you live in the country it is likely that your roses may be harmed at some time by rabbits, deer and farm animals grazing in fields adjacent to gardens. I have also heard of squirrels damaging roses.

Rabbits love to nibble at young succulent shoots and can be a major problem, preventing young plants from assuming proper growth and causing older ones to be bare at the base. Control of rabbits is almost impossible because they breed so quickly. If they cannot be kept out of the garden, you will need to put protection of some sort around your roses, at least near the base.

Deer and grazing animals also enjoy the flavour of roses and if you have them growing as a boundary, either as a hedge or in the form of climbers and ramblers on fences, they are likely to be at risk. Deer are likely to strike in midwinter when they are most hungry. The only

Above: Leaf-rolling sawflies lay their eggs on the surface of the leaf which then becomes curled as protection for the eggs.

precaution is to plant the thorniest of varieties, but these can still be at risk if the animals are hungry enough.

Moles can also be a danger to roses, especially if they are present in large numbers, by tunnelling under roots and damaging them. There are several ways of ridding the garden of moles and it may be worth trying one of the old-fashioned methods. The most popular is to put an empty bottle in the tunnel beneath a molehill. The sound of the wind blowing across the top of the bottle is said to upset the moles.

Other rose ailments

Viruses

Viruses are transmitted at the time of propagation and have nothing to do with the husbandry of the rose in the garden. It is more likely that the rootstock used during propagation years ago infected a variety, and that this variety has gone on to be the strain available today. The majority of growers use rootstock grown from seed, which by and large prevents the spread of viruses to offspring, but if the budded cultivar had already been infected, there is no prevention and the newly resulting rose plant will share the same traits.

Exactly what these are, no one can be sure. The most prevalent symptoms of virus are irregularities in the leaf, for example wavy yellow lines across the surface, but flower quality can be affected too. Malcolm Manners, of the Citrus Institute, Florida Southern College, USA, who has worked on this subject, has produced virus-free forms of the older roses we love, with stunningly larger flowers than would be expected, perhaps true to their original form.

It is often the case that a rose will appear perfectly healthy for a large part of its life but with no warning will suddenly show signs of having a virus. It is this occurrence that led to the belief that viruses were some sort of contagious problem, but we can be sure that viruses are not spread in the way fungal diseases are. As this is the case, there is no reason to worry about a rose with the problem, it is simply a case of having to live with it.

Proliferation

Proliferated flowers can cause much alarm when seen for the first time. Some of the old-fashioned double roses will develop an extra bud or buds from the centre of the flower.These buds will be seen to be perfect examples and will often be attached to a short stem from the centre of the flower.

The cause of this malformation is uncertain; some say that it is a virus and others that it is some genetic mutation; what is more certain is that there are factors that affect its severity. Plants grown in shady places seem to suffer more than those grown in more open places or under glass. The problem also seems to occur more often after a cold spring. Repeat-flowering varieties seldom show signs of it in their second flush, so the only treatment for these is to remove the offensive blooms that appear earlier in the year and wait for later ones to arrive.

Balled flowers

Balling of flowers usually occurs when there has been rain followed by sun, or when the atmosphere is generally damp. Outer petals on full-flowered roses become fused together when wet and the effect of the sun is to cook the damp petals so that they form a shell

Below: Proliferation is a malformation of the flowers usually seen early in the flowering season.

Above: The tinest droplet of weedkiller can seriously disfigure rose leaves. Always avoid spraying weedkiller near roses if there is a breeze.

around the flower. If no action is taken, all the petals will eventually turn brown and the flower will fall to the ground. If you have time and perhaps only a few affected roses, the outer petals can be gently teased open to allow the remainder of the flower to form naturally.

Chlorosis

Yellowing and the appearance of pale patches on the leaf are often caused by mineral deficiencies; usually, iron and magnesium are the elements responsible. To ensure the well-being of the rose, an attempt should be made to correct the situation. Yellowing foliage suggests that the plant is probably suffering from iron deficiency. An application of sequestered iron or a feed of liquid seaweed with added iron will usually redress the situation.

Epsom salts are available from most chemists and will cure magnesium deficiency, which causes leaves to develop pale patches between the veins.

Spray damage

Although largely common sense, it is useful to include a word about spray damage. Roses are very susceptible to even the tiniest amounts of weedkiller, and if this is used in the garden it should be applied when there is little or no breeze to prevent it drifting on to garden roses. Always use a separate sprayer for this purpose; no matter how well it is washed out there are always minor traces left, enough to cause damage. Of course, if spraying is being carried out in adjacent fields you will have no control over drifting and the resulting damage will manifest itself in the form of distorted growth, and in very bad cases even death of the plant.

Scorch

Scorch on rose leaves is more unsightly than of any great detriment to the plant. It is likely to be more apparent on roses growing under cover that have been placed too close to the glass or polythene, or that have had their leaves watered. Outside it can occur when there has been full sun after rain, but this is less likely. Leaves will become brown and papery around their edges, and if badly affected will fall. If watering roses with a hose or can, try to do so in the morning or evening when the sun's rays are less powerful.

Below: Leaves can easily become scorched if there is very hot sun after rain. Dark red and deep pink flowers can fade in strong sunlight. This rose, 'Souvenir du Docteur Jamain', is best planted in the shade.

Plant directory

Classification of rose types

The genus *Rosa* is a hugely complicated one, but a total understanding of its complexity is not needed to appreciate the merits of individual roses. A breakdown of the various groups can help to compare the value of one group with another, so for the purposes of this directory I have classified them into 'family' groups, where those in each group are in some way related and similar in habit and form. One group may be closely related to another but, although this may occasionally be apparent, is not especially relevant when it comes to selecting roses for the garden.

This directory is divided first according to the nature of the roses, into bush, shrub, climbing and rambling roses, then, within each of these headings, into the family groups contained there. Many of the older groups have a name that refers in some way to one of the original species roses from which the group developed. Recently, however, the name given refers more to the style of the roses in that group; or, in the case of a diverse group, they are referred to using a broader title, such as the Modern Shrub roses. It would be almost impossible to describe every rose in existence, but included in each group are the most important, both in garden worthiness and their role in the group. Although not every member of the group is described, I have included where possible a cross-section of varieties to show the choice available.

Flowering seasons

In all descriptions, reference is made to the flowering season. As a guide, summer-flowering roses produce one abundant flush of blooms, repeat-flowering varieties will provide more than one flush and continuous-flowering varieties will flower intermittently throughout the season. The date of introduction is given where known and in all cases the size given is height before spread. Sizes are for an average mature plant; it may be that soil and climate differences cause the rose to vary from the sizes stated.

Bush or bedding roses

These generally fall into two categories, Hybrid Teas and Floribundas, although there are many roses described in the shrub section that can be used in the same way as these. They are not so fashionable now, but these are the roses used in large beds of single or mixed varieties and in other more formal planting. They are also useful in tubs or in mixed planting in borders. Hybrid Teas and Floribundas are often referred to as modern roses, but the definition of modern roses is controversial. Some consider that the date of introduction of the first Hybrid Tea 'La France' should be the point from which the modern rose dates, but this was in 1865 and I personally do not think that everything from 1865 can be described as modern. My preference is to use the Second World War as a cut-off date, the convention used by several eminent rosarians.

Hybrid Teas or Large-flowered roses

Two titles are applied to this group of roses. Early Hybrid Teas were, indeed, hybrids of the Tea roses, but over the years their genealogy has become more complicated, leading to a new name of Large-flowered roses, however I like many find it difficult to think of them as anything but Hybrid Teas. They are a huge group of roses and remain extremely popular

Above: Although 'Fragrant Cloud' was introduced in 1964, it is still very popular today.

with gardeners. They are ideal for cutting as they usually bear solitary blooms, although a few produce small clusters. Among them can be found colours for every taste, and many exude a perfume. They are a useful group of roses that are usually quite bushy and free flowering. There are also some climbing Hybrid Teas described later in this directory.

'Anna Pavlova'

This variety has a most delicious perfume that is almost overpowering. Full blooms are soft blush pink from pointed buds and leaves are leathery dark green and rounded in shape. It is tall for a Hybrid Tea and can be quite slender. Try to avoid planting it in poor soil or shade.

Beales, UK, 1981, continuous flowering, 1.2 x 1 m (4 x 3 ft)

'Fragrant Cloud'

The double orangey red flowers of this Hybrid Tea are deeply scented. Foliage is dark and glossy, with plum-coloured young shoots. An upright growing variety.

Tantau, Germany 1964, Continuous flowering, 75 x 60 cm (30 x 24 ft)

'Just Joey'

The flowers on this rose are large, and blowsy and petals are wavy edged. Its coppery orange

colouring makes it stand out in the garden, where it is very free flowering. Leaves are dark and glossy, if a little sparse and growth is strong. This is an excellent rose.

Cant, UK, 1972, continuous flowering, 60 x 60 cm (24 x 24 in)

'La France'

I include this as it was the first of its type to be introduced, although it is no more outstanding than many other Hybrid Teas. Full flowers are mid-silvery pink and are very highly perfumed. It displays upright growth, which carries mid-green leaves.

Guillot Fils, France, 1865, repeat flowering, 1.2 x 1 m (4 x 3 ft)

'Mrs Oakley Fisher'

Several single varieties were introduced in the early part of the 20th century and this is one of my favourites. The flowers are best described as apricot with a bold ring of bright orange stamens. Young growth and leaves are plum coloured, a beautiful contrast to the flowers.

Cant, UK, 1921, continuous flowering, 60 x 60 cm (24 x 24 in)

'Ophelia'

'Ophelia' is one of the most beautiful older Hybrid Teas. The fully double, pointed blooms are soft creamy pink with a tinge of lemon at the base and are scented. When open, the flower displays a magnificent circle of amber gold stamens. Foliage is large and leathery. Also similar are 'Lady Sylvia' and 'Mme Butterfly', both sports of it.

W. Paul, 1912, continuous flowering 60 x 60 cm (24 x 24 in)

'Royal William'

Deep velvety red, fully double blooms are well scented and remain high centred even when fully open. A good rose for cutting, on an upright plant with plentiful dark green foliage.

Kordes, Germany, 1984, continuous flowering, 75 x 60 cm (30 x 24 in)

Floribundas or Cluster-flowered roses

As with the Hybrid Teas, Floribundas have also been given a new title, but I find 'Cluster-flowered roses' much more cumbersome than 'Floribundas' so I shall stick with this. Perhaps these words will roll off the tongues of future generations with ease. These roses, by whatever name you give them, are free flowering and support masses of blooms in clusters. They are ideal for mass planting but have other uses as well. They are successful if planted in tubs or in mixed planting with other shrubs and perennials, and the longer stemmed varieties are also good as cut blooms.

'Amber Queen'

This is an excellent little rose and, judging by the number of awards it has received, I am not alone in this opinion. Many-petalled blooms are golden amber amid dark, glossy leaves on a bushy plant. This shorter growing Floribunda is at home anywhere in the garden and will be happy in a tub or at the front of the border.
Harkness, UK, 1984, continuous flowering, 60 x 60 cm (24 x 24 in)

'Korresia'

Bright, clear yellow blooms are well sized and held in large clusters. Leaves are large and healthy, glossy mid-green. 'Korresia' is a stocky, sturdily growing plant.
Kordes, Germany, 1977, continuous flowering, 60 x 60 cm (24 x 24 in)

'Lili Marlene'

Double flowers are cupped and open, rich velvety red with bright anthers. It is very free flowering, producing its blooms in large clusters. It does not get huge and makes a good specimen in a small tub. Growth is bushy with well-armed stems, and leaves are dark leathery green.
Kordes, Germany, 1959, continuous flowering, 60 x 75 cm (24 x 30 in)

'Margaret Merril'

White flowers are gently flushed pink. Buds are very pointed until the bloom opens, when pronounced golden anthers are revealed. A special feature of this lovely rose is its superb perfume. Foliage is dark and growth upright.
Harkness, UK, 1977, continuous flowering, 75 x 60 cm (30 x 24 in)

'Norwich Castle'

Flowers are a lovely shade of coppery orange and are double, opening flat and fading to a soft apricot orange as they mature. Leaves are light to mid-green and growth is upright in habit. A very free-flowering variety.
Beales, UK, 1979, continuous flowering, 75 x 60 cm (30 x 24 in)

'Plentiful'

Although a modern rose, the style of the flowers is old fashioned. They are packed with

Below: 'Lili Marlene' produces abundant flowers with a velvety texture.

Above: 'Twenty-fifth' is an excellent all-round bedding rose.

Miniature and patio roses

Patio roses

The name Patio rose was given to a group of roses that are really just compact Floribundas, with the intention of making gardeners aware that roses can be grown in a pot on the patio. This group of roses make good specimens in tubs but they are not the only ones with this capability; all roses, even vigorous ramblers, can be grown in a pot with some degree of success, provided they are well fed and watered. Patio roses can also be grown elsewhere in the garden, at the front of the border or as a specimen plant in a small garden.

very deep pink petals, which form a quartered appearance. Leaves are leathery, a little coarse and dark green in colour. A thorny plant.
LeGrice, UK, 1961, continuous flowering, 75 x 75 cm (30 x 30 in)

'Queen Elizabeth'
'Queen Elizabeth' is one of the most famous of all Floribundas. Everything about it is big: the flowers, leaves and growth are all larger than average. Double flowers emerge from long pointed buds and are soft clear pink with a little perfume; they are arranged in clusters. The large leaves are dark and glossy, and the growth is upright and tall for its type. 'Queen Elizabeth' makes a good hedge or boundary in places where it is not possible to accommodate a wide hedge.
Lammerts, USA, 1954, continuous flowering, 1.5 x 75 cm (5 ft x 30 in)

'Twenty-fifth'
This variety produces masses of deep blood red, semi-double, open flowers in large clusters regularly throughout the summer months. Each open bloom displays a fine coronet of golden yellow stamens. Foliage is dark, glossy and clean. A healthy and useful little rose.
Beales, UK, 1996, continuous flowering, 60 x 60 cm (24 x 24 in)

'Apricot Sunblaze'
This rose has a dense habit with small glossy leaves. Bright orange red blooms, which are at first cupped, open flat and display many petals. They are mostly borne in clusters although it is possible to find the odd single flower.
Saville, USA, 1984, continuous flowering, 38 x 25 cm (15 x 10 in)

'Dresden Doll'
Soft pink flowers are semi-double, cupped and emerge from heavily mossed buds in clusters. Stems are also covered in moss which, if touched, is slightly scented. This is a compact and unusual rose.
Moore, USA, 1975, continuous flowering, 30 x 25 cm (12 x 10 in)

'Regensberg'
Large double flowers are bright cerise-pink with white streaks and edging and at their centres. The reverse of the petals is also silvery white. It is one of the so-called 'hand-painted' roses for which this breeder is well known.
McGredy, New Zealand, 1979, continuous flowering, 45 x 45 cm (18 x 18 in)

'Robin Redbreast'

Semi-double red flowers have central creamy white centres and appear in bunches in great profusion throughout the summer. Leaves are glossy and mid-green on thorny stems. Inclined to spreading growth.

Ilsink, Netherlands, 1984, continuous flowering , 45 x 45 cm (18 x 18 in)

'Sweet Dream'

Soft peachy apricot blooms are double and prettily formed in a cupped style. Usually borne in clusters, there may be a few single blooms. Dense, very glossy foliage; reasonably resistant to disease. Growth compact.

Fryer, UK, 1988, continuous flowering, 45 x 30 cm (18 x 12 in)

Miniature roses

Miniatures were popular at the beginning of the 19th century, but there were few colours available at this time and they soon became unfashionable. Cultivation of them ceased until the 1920s when 'Rouletii' was discovered in Switzerland, and so began a new era of popularity in which new Miniatures were raised. It is best to purchase Miniatures that have been developed on their own roots, as these roses will be smaller than their equivalent counterparts that have been budded or grafted. Although often sold as houseplants they do not respond well to being grown indoors. They can be successful in window boxes or as edging to both beds and borders.

'Cinderella'

A pretty little rose of white flushed pink. Small flowers are very double against tiny light green leaves. One of the best of the Miniatures, with dense and compact growth.

de Vink, Netherlands, 1953, continuous flowering, 30 x 25 cm (12 x 10 in)

'Easter Morning'

Fully double, creamy white flowers with hints of lemon. Fragrant. Leaves are dark green, providing a contrasting foil for the flowers. Dense growth; inclined to be broad in habit.

Moore, USA, 1960, continuous flowering, 30 x 30 cm (12 x 12 in)

'Hula Girl'

Pointed buds open to reveal double flowers of bright orange to salmon pink with just a touch of yellow at the base of the petals. Profuse blooms over a long period. Glossy foliage.

Williams, USA, 1975, continuous flowering, 30 x 30 cm (12 x 12 in)

'June Time'

Flowers are mid-pink with a deeper pink reverse and are very double, borne in small clusters. Foliage is dark and glossy and reasonably resistant to disease. Growth is dense and spreading.

Moore, USA, 1963, continuous flowering, 30 x 30 cm (12 x 12 in)

Shrub roses

There are very many shrub roses all of differing nature, there are summer-flowering varieties and those that flower well into the autumn. Some set hips, some double as small climbers,

Below: 'Alba Maxima' has typical green grey Alba foliage.

some will be content to remain at knee height, and others will grow above the height of any person. Colours vary from white to deep purple, some have single flowers while others are very, very double, some are scented and some not. So it goes on. Between themselves, shrub roses are individual but within their groups they share similarities, in both habit and flower form. Although the group to which they belong is not the ultimate factor in choosing one variety against another, the characteristics of each group will, if understood, aid in the decision. Their uses are diverse, from mixed and specimen planting to growing in tubs.

Albas

Dating back to the 15th century, the Albas are one of the oldest races of the rose available today. They have characteristic grey green leaves and pastel-shaded flowers, the deepest colouring being mid-silvery pink, and they are refined in their beauty. They are highly perfumed and bloom *en masse* in midsummer. They are a very healthy bunch, matt leaves seeming to deter the unwanted spores of disease. 'Alba Maxima' with its double white flowers is said by some to be the White Rose of York adopted by Edward Duke of York, later to be Edward IV, as the symbol of his house on defeating the Lancastrians at Mortimer's Cross in 1461. It was an Alba rose 'Maiden's Blush' that caught the attention of my father as a child and stimulated his interest in roses, a genus which would go on to become his life's preoccupation. Without his inspiration it is possible that I never would have appreciated the rose.

Above: 'Alba Semiplena' produces hips in the autumn.

'Alba Maxima'

Also known as 'Jacobite Rose' and 'White Rose of York'. This rose is one of the candidates put forward as being the 'White Rose of York', although expert opinion suggests that this was actually *Rosa alba*. Double, infurled flowers are white, occasionally flushed with cream or, when grown in shade, blush pink, with a lovely refined perfume. They appear in clusters against very deep grey green leaves and thorny upright stems. Will sometime set hips that are ovoid in shape.

Of unknown origin, 15th century or before, summer flowering, 1.8 x 1.2 m (6 x 4 ft)

'Alba Semiplena'

Semi-double flowers are pure white, slightly cupped, have a coronet of bright golden anthers and are sweetly scented. Foliage is dark grey green and matt. This Alba will produce a good display of hips in the autumn.

Of unknown origin, likely to be 16th century or before, summer flowering, 2.5 x 1.5 m (8 x 5 ft)

'Celestial'

Also known as 'Celeste', this is a beautiful rose with saucer-shaped semi-double soft pink blooms. These are scented and dominate the plant in profusion for two or three weeks in summer. Their brief appearance is complemented by soft grey green leaves that make up for their absence later in the season. The perfume exuded by the flowers is strong yet unpretentious. This is also a good rose as far as growth habit and disease resistance are concerned.

Of unknown origin, very old, summer flowering, 1.8 x 1.2 m (6 x 4 ft)

'Königin von Dänemark'

Also known as 'Queen of Denmark', this variety has perhaps the deepest colouring of the Albas, being rich to silvery pink. The flowers, which are perhaps a little smaller than that of its relations, are heavily scented and fully double. Leaves, although of similar colouring are tougher in appearance.

Booth, Denmark, 1826, summer flowering, 1.5 x 1.2 m (5 x 4 ft)

'Mme Legras de St Germain'

Flowers are a little smaller than the majority of Albas, creamy white and perfumed and produced abundantly in clusters. Foliage is soft grey green with few thorns. This is a vigorous member of its group and, if grown on a wall, will attain greater height than if it is grown as a free-standing shrub.

Early 19th century, summer flowering, 2.1 x 1.8 m (7 x 6 ft)

'Maiden's Blush Great'

This is a beautiful rose with wonderfully perfumed blush pink, double flowers and soft grey green leaves. In France it is called 'Cuisse de Nymphe', meaning thigh of the nymph, but this was too much for the Victorians in England who renamed it.

Of unknown origin, likely to be from the 15th century or before, summer flowering 1.8 x 1.5 m (6 x 5 ft)

Bourbons

The Bourbons take their name from an island in the southern Indian Ocean, Ile de Bourbon (now called Réunion). In habit this is a varying group, from plants of around a metre through to larger shrubs which are also suitable as small climbers with support, to vigorous climbers. (The climbers are described on page 101.) The flowers, in many shades from white to deep purple-reds, are usually perfumed, some of them very strongly, and are generally double in formation. Most repeat or continue to flower throughout the summer months and often into autumn as well. They have glossy leaves with medium-sized oval leaflets. There are some excellent and some very famous varieties to be found among the ranks of the Bourbons.

'Boule de Neige'

As the name implies, the white petals of this lovely flower reflex to form a globular flower. Sometimes tinged with a purplish red when in bud, they are highly scented. Leaves are dark and glossy. Repeats well in the right situation.

Lacharme, France, 1867, repeat flowering, 1.2 x 1 m (4 x 3 ft)

'Commandant Beaurepaire'

An elegant striped variety with large flowers streaked and marbled with pink, white and purple, scented and with golden anthers at their centres. Leaves are long and pointed, mid-green in colour. 'Commandant Beaurepaire' will tolerate some shade, where its unusual colouring will be most resplendent. A good rose, well worth considering if a striped rose is desired.

Moreau-Robert, France, 1874, repeat flowering, 1.5 x 1.5 m (5 x 5 ft)

'Gipsy Boy'

This is a lax shrub rose that can also double as a climber. Flowers are not huge but double, crimson purple and scented, putting on a mass display in season. Slightly wrinkled mid-green leaves clothe the shrub amply. This is a vigorous rose producing new canes of growth throughout the summer. Often sets hips.

Lambert, Germany, 1909, summer flowering, 1.8 x 1.2 m (6 x 4 ft)

'Louise Odier'

An excellent rose. From round tight buds emerge highly scented, fully double, cupped flowers of mid-silvery pink. As they mature they become flatter, exposing the anthers and slightly ragged inner petals that are often tinged with lilac. With regular dead-heading flowers will be produced regularly throughout the summer. Arching growth can be encouraged to climb when this variety is grown near a wall.

Margottin, France, 1851, continuous flowering, 1.5 x 1.2 m (5 x 4 ft)

'Mme Isaac Pereire'

The colour of the huge blowsy blooms of 'Mme Isaac Pereire' is best described as purplish pink, which fades in hot sun. The perfume they emit is heady and powerful. Long arching canes of growth make it well suited to climbing – as the heavy blooms are inclined to nod down, they can be better appreciated if higher up. Early blooms are sometimes prone to proliferation, but there will be many more to follow so this should not be considered too much of a drawback. Leaves are large, pointed and maroon edged.

Garçon, France, 1881, continuous flowering, 2.1 x 1.5 m (7 x 5 ft)

'Mme Pierre Oger'

Like the rose from which it sported ,'La Reine Victoria', this also has cupped double blooms borne in clusters that remain globular for much of their life. They are soft delicate pink with the

Above: 'Mme Isaac Pereire' has an outstanding perfume.

colour intensified in shade, and highly perfumed. This is a rose of superior form and beauty and for this it is very popular. Leaves are pointed, mid-green and, sadly, rather prone to disease later in the season, but this should not deter you from choosing it if you spray for such problems.

Verdier, France, 1878, continuous flowering, 1.2 x 1.2 m (4 x 4 ft)

'Souvenir de la Malmaison'

This is a truly beautiful rose with large, flat, quartered blooms of soft blush pink with a wonderful perfume. They appear repeatedly throughout the summer on a strongly growing plant. The only drawback is a tendency to ball in wet weather, but the outer petals can be teased open to allow the flower to emerge naturally. It is said that in 1814 Empress Josephine handed a bloom of a rose to Tsar Alexander, Emperor of Russia, saying 'Un souvenir de la Malmaison'. Later when visiting France, the Grand Duke of Russia recalled these words and suggested that the name be given to a seedling rose sent to Malmaison by the breeder Beluze and this lovely rose is it.

Beluze, France, 1943, continuous flowering, 1.8 x 1.8 m (6 x 6 ft)

Centifolias

Also known as Provence roses or Cabbage roses, Centifolias are the 'roses of a hundred petals' and date from the 15th and 16th centuries. They are the large blowsy-bloomed roses (the reason for their other name of Cabbage roses) so often portrayed in the paintings of the Old Masters, particularly the Dutch and Flemish painters, which is understandable as it was the Dutch breeders of that era who carried out much pioneering work in the introduction of new varieties. Some of them can be difficult to situate in the garden, as they are a little cumbersome in growth. If you have the space to cope with long, arching branches, the larger varieties will reward you with abundant beautiful, shaggy, highly perfumed blooms but they will require some support. The smaller Centifolias, however, are often quite neat with flowers more in proportion with their size.

'Blanchefleur'

The flowers, which are a little smaller than some of its group, are white sometimes edged pink, double and open flat, exuding a delightful scent. They appear in bunches in abundance. It is more compact than many of its relations, with grey green soft foliage. It is tolerant of poor soils and will brighten a shaded place, which it will cope with reasonably well.

Vibert, France, 1835, summer flowering, 1.5 x 1.2 m (5 x 4 ft)

'Fantin Latour'

This is one of the most beautiful of the Centifolias. Its flowers are full, flat and quartered, soft powder pink with, in my opinion, a sumptuous perfume. It has attractive deepish green, rounded foliage and strong arching growth. Although clearly named for the famous artist, Henri Fantin Latour, little more is known of its origin.

Probably 19th century, summer flowering, 1.5 x 1.2 m (5 x 4 ft)

'Rose de Meaux'

This is one of the tidiest and most compact-growing Centifolias. Its growth is upright and short. Flowers are semi-double, cupped and in ratio to the size of the plant, soft to mid-pink. Leaves are also small, pointed and grey green. A lovely little rose that is useful near the front of a border or in a tub.

Sweet, UK, before 1789, summer flowering, 60 x 60 cm (24 x 24 in)

'Tour de Malakoff'

Big blowsy flowers are bright magenta pink when at their peak and fade slowly through shades of purple to lilac grey. They have a super perfume. The plant itself is lax and vigorous and will often benefit from support. Sometimes called the 'Taffeta Rose'.

Soupert and Notting, Luxembourg, 1856, summer flowering, 1.5 x 1.2 m (5 x 4 ft)

'White Provence'

Also known as 'Unique Blanche'. The growth of this rose can often be unruly but, although they hate wet weather, the flowers can truly compensate. Creamy white with a sheen to the petals, they appear slightly later than many once-flowering varieties and give away a lovely perfume; this is a true connoisseur's variety.

Found in UK ,1775, summer flowering, 1.5 x 1.2 m (5 x 4 ft)

Chinas

As their name suggests, these roses originally derived from China, where it is believed that they existed as far back as the 10th century, even before. They are important in the history of the rose as they are largely responsible for the long flowering period of most of today's modern roses. They cover a wide palette of colour and range of habits, and many of them are perfumed. They are suited to bedding,

Above: 'Cécile Brunner' (shown twice life size) has clusters
of dainty flowers.

specimen or container planting, but they are
not on the whole hardy roses and may need
protection in colder areas during the winter
months. They are rewarding cool greenhouse
or conservatory plants.

'Cécile Brunner'

Also known as 'Sweetheart Rose'. The
individual flowers are not huge and stunning,
more elegant and delicate, but when blooming
en masse they are collectively lovely. Small,
shell pink and pointed in bud, they open in a
slightly ragged style on the end of long stems in
clusters. The long flower stem makes them
ideal for buttonholes. The plant is not overly
endowed with foliage, individual leaves are
slender and growth is a little awkward. Having
said this, 'Cécile Brunner' is a good all-round
rose. There are also white and climbing forms.

Pernet Ducher, France, 1881, continuous flowering,
1.2 m x 60 cm (4 ft x 24 in)

'Old Blush'

This is also known as 'Parson's Pink'. It is an important rose in that it was used in breeding programmes very early on, and is largely the reason for the remontant qualities in today's hybrids. It was discovered growing in China and had reached Europe by the 1780s, and is still worthy of inclusion in the garden today. Semi-double open flowers are mid-silvery pink and scented. This large shrub rose can be grown as a climber if it is provided with some support.

Parson, China, continuous flowering, 1.8 x 1.2 m (6 x 4 ft)

'Mutabilis'

This must be one of the most characteristically individual roses of all. Single flowers, when fresh, are a blend of many different shades including apricot, yellow, orange, pink and red, but almost invariably with age settling on a shade of raspberry pink. This may sound peculiar but the effect is quite stunning; this rose has to be one of my favourites, not for its uniqueness, although this has some relevance but because it makes a truly fantastic sight. Young growth is plum coloured, which adds to its crazy palette. In some situations it will remain relatively dwarf, in others it will do its best to climb.

China, 1932, continuous flowering, 1.2 x 1 m (4 x 3 ft)

'Perle d'Or'

Very much like 'Cécile Brunner', although I prefer the colouring of this being buff to apricot with pink tinges. Flowers are held on long stems in clusters. Growth is a little less angular but still somewhat awkward, a typical China trait. Stems are almost thorn free and foliage is dark. 'Perle d'Or' enjoys good conditions and in the most favourable it will grow taller than stated here.

Dubreuil, France, 1884, continuous flowering, 1.2 m x 60 cm (4 ft x 24 in)

'Sophie's Perpetual'

I hesitated to include this variety in the shrub section of this directory, but have settled on doing so as it will only attain useful climbing size in very good conditions. Having said this, be prepared for it to outgrow the suggested size once its roots find welcoming soil. I am a fan of this rose which, while perhaps not possessing the most beautiful of flowers, has a lovely perfume and is generally healthy. Individually the flowers are double, faint pink and heavily edged with cherry cerise. This is a free-flowering clustered variety.

Re-introduced in 1960, UK, continuous flowering, 2.5 x 1.2 m (8 x 4 ft)

'Viridiflora'

Also known as 'Green Rose'. I could not leave this variety out as it is such a peculiarity. Blooms are almost deformed, with normal petals replaced by green, brown-tinged bracts, that become purplish brown as they mature. This is a rose for the collector or flower arranger with a sense of humour. Generally healthy and easy to grow.

Of unknown origin, but around 1833, continuous flowering, 1 x 1 m (3 x 3 ft)

Below: 'Quatre Saisons' is typical of the Damasks famed for their perfume.

Damasks

The Damasks are known to have been around in Roman and Ancient Greek times. In the Middle East they were prized for their scent and were used for the extraction of attar or oil of roses to produce perfume. The exact timing of their arrival in Europe is unknown but it was certainly many, many years ago. Although not a huge number of them exist, they are beautiful roses, ranging from mid-pink to white in colour and generally scented. Most flower just once but there are one or two exceptions, in particular 'Quatre Saisons' which has a good second flush of flowers. In fact it was this rose that allowed the Roman pagan festival of Rosalia, which was held first in early summer, to be repeated in early autumn.

Above: 'Mme Hardy' has a significant green eye at the centre of the flower.

'Ispahan'

This rose flowers for a long season. The very fragrant flowers are double and well shaped with reflexed petals, unfading mid- to soft pink. The shrub is strong in growth with mid-green leaves and is relatively free of thorns.

Middle East, probably Persia, before 1832, summer flowering, 1.2 x 1 m (4 x 3 ft)

'Kazanlik'

Bearing the name of one of the centres of the perfume industry in the Middle East of its time, this is a wonderful, deliciously perfumed Damask rose. Slightly shaggy, double to semi-double flowers are warm mid-pink, fading just a little as they age. A good shrub specimen that may need some support in the garden.

Middle East, date of origin unknown, summer flowering, 1.5 x 1.2 m (5 x 4 ft)

'Léda'

Also known as 'Painted Damask'. It is clear to see why this rose has been given its second name, for its pure white flowers are edged with crimson, almost as though someone had painstakingly touched them up with a brush and paint. Individually the flowers have reflexed outer petals and infurled central ones, giving them a rounded shape. They are scented and borne on a tidy, generally healthy plant.

Probably early 19th century, summer flowering, 1.5 x 1 m (5 x 3 ft)

'Mme Hardy'

A famous old variety. White flowers are double and of good size, exposing at their centres a distinctive green eye, and are scented. Once settled this rose can produce a good number of exquisite blooms, almost obliterating its foliage. Strong growth is relatively tidy and produces bright green, slightly glossy foliage

Hardy, France, 1832, summer flowering, 1.5 x 1.5 m (5 x 5 ft)

'Quatre Saisons'

Also known as 'Autumn Damask'. The flowers appear, unusually for this group, in two flushes. They are mid- to soft pink, double, ragged in formation, highly scented and good for making pot-pourri. An unkempt plant in many ways, it produces early autumn flowers on the growth made in the summer of the same year, which must be borne in mind during pruning.

Middle East, very old, summer flowering, 1.2 x 1 m (4 x 3 ft)

Above: *Rosa Mundi* dates back to the 12th century.

Gallicas

The crusaders of the 12th and 13th centuries brought specimens and seeds of roses from the east to Europe and it is likely that many of these were Gallicas. During the Middle Ages, the chemists of the time used many roses in the treatment of various ailments, and the famous *Rosa gallica officinallis* was one of the varieties they most frequently depended on, in fact it is often listed today as the 'Apothecary's Rose'. It is also the Red Rose of Lancaster adopted by Henry IV as the symbol of his house and made famous due to the Wars of

the Roses. Later, these roses found favour with the Empress Josephine, who is said to have collected more than 150 varieties in her garden at the Château Malmaison. In habit they are strong growing and tough, most are perfumed, and in colour they range from soft shades of pink to deep purples and maroons. The flowers are diverse in shape, anything from single to large and fully double. On the whole they are tidy and not too well endowed with thorns. They are usually tolerant of poor soil and shade, flowering in great abundance in midsummer, and are at home almost anywhere. When grown on their own roots, Gallicas will sucker freely. There are some beautiful members of this group, and no rose garden is complete with out at least one.

'Belle de Crécy'

Medium-sized flowers are lilac purple, fading to grey as they mature. Although this colour is different to the majority of roses, there are some of similar colouring that surpass this one, but it is easier to place in the garden than some of these due to its reasonable size. Having said this, when the weather is good, so are the flowers and they are well scented. Growth is upright and almost free of thorns.

Hardy, France, 1829, summer flowering, 1.2 x 1 m (4 x 3 ft)

'Cardinal de Richelieu'

From tight buds of magenta red emerge fully double flowers of rich purple. The central petals are furled inwards, demonstrating their lighter reverse and hiding the stamens. They are deliciously perfumed and are held in clusters. The foliage is silky and dark green, often edged with maroon when young. Few thorns.

Laffay, France, 1840, summer flowering, 1.2 x 1 m (4 x 3 ft)

'Charles de Mills'

This is a famous old cultivar and everyone's favourite when in full flush. The large blooms when open are broad mushroom shaped and almost perfectly round, consisting of very many petals. In colour they are a mixture of maroon and purple, overall somewhere between the two. I find this rose heavily scented but others find it almost devoid of perfume. Foliage is dark on smooth stems.

Of unknown origin, an old variety, summer flowering, 1.2 x 1.2 m (4 x 4 ft)

'Duchesse de Montebello'

A beautiful rose. Flowers are fully double, soft, clear and bright pink with a sweet perfume. Inner petals furl inwards around a bright green eye and, when open, they are the shape of a shallow dish. Foliage is relatively healthy and dark, new growth is lavish and almost cane-like. 'Duchesse de Montebello' will tolerate poor soils and shade to some extent.

Laffay, France, 1829, summer flowering, 1.2 x 1 m (4 x 3 ft)

'Empress Josephine'

Named in honour of the Empress, this is a truly lovely rose. Wavy petals make up the slightly ragged flowers which are, in essence, deep pink, but heavy veining and tinges of blush and occasionally lilac give them a softer appearance. They are scented. A somewhat lax grower yet well foliated. Generally tolerant of all but the worst conditions.

Of unknown origin, thought to be early 19th century, summer flowering, 1.5 x 1.2 m (5 x 4 ft)

'James Mason'

A relatively recent addition to the Gallicas, this is a stunning rose, created by my father. When breeding it he relied on the red colouring and health of 'Scharlachglüt', a shrub/climbing rose of the 1950s, and the qualities of the wonderful 'Tuscany Superb' to supply its offspring with the best of both parents, and this they did. The flowers are abundant in midsummer, semi-double, carmine red, with a velvety sheen and a bold coronet of bright golden anthers. They are large, lightly scented and slightly cupped with the odd petal reflexing backwards. Foliage is dark and leathery, clothing the plant well.

Beales, UK, 1982, summer flowering, 1.5 x 1.2 m (5 x 4 ft)

'Tuscany Superb'

I had to include this beautiful rose. Flowers are medium in size, semi-double and possess a very heady fragrance. In colour they are rich purple red, and velvety both in sheen and to the touch; open and flat, they display contrasting golden anthers. Foliage is dark green and generally healthy, growth upright.

Paul, UK, 1848, summer flowering, 1.2 x 1 m (4 x 3 ft)

Hybrid Musks

These were the first tidy, continuous-flowering shrub roses, originally classified as Hybrid Teas and then called Pemberton roses after the Rev. Joseph Pemberton, who bred them between 1913 and 1926. He bred some excellent varieties that are still popular today. The majority of Hybrid Musks were created by Pemberton but a few were introduced after his death and many of these are still with us also. Although the majority produce their blooms in clusters, individually they vary in colour and form, from creamy white single blooms to flamboyant red and fully double. Most are scented. They are useful garden plants; the smaller varieties adapt well to growing in tubs while some of the taller varieties will grow as small climbers when positioned against a wall. Most will even suffer shade and poor soil.

'Ballerina'

This is an outstanding rose. Flowers are small and single in large clusters, pink with white centres. They appear continuously, especially if the plant is regularly dead-headed, through the summer and into the autumn. Leaves are narrow and plentiful. 'Ballerina' is excellent when grown in a tub.

Bentall, UK, 1937, continuous flowering, 1.2 x 1 m (4 x 3 ft)

'Buff Beauty'

The flowers of this variety vary in colour from one garden to another, from soft buff to bright apricot orange, largely due to the soil and amount of sun. They are double, scented and appear in clusters. Leaves are dark green and glossy. The growth can be vigorous and spreading, allowing this rose to be grown as a small climber with support if desired.

Bentall, UK, 1939, continuous flowering, 1.5 x 1.5 m (5 x 5 ft)

Left: The flowers of 'Penelope' open out flat from peachy pink buds.

Above: 'Felicia' is very free flowering.

'Felicia'

One of the most lovely Hybrid Musks. Medium-sized, double flowers are soft pink with hints of salmon and are nicely scented. Slightly deeper blooms appear in early autumn. A plant of reasonable vigour and health with dark, slightly crinkled foliage.

Pemberton, UK, 1928, continuous flowering, 1.2 x 1.2 m (4 x 4 ft)

'Moonlight'

The small flowers are semi-double, creamy white, with a tinge of yellow and golden stamens; they are borne in large clusters of buds and open blooms. Foliage is dark and healthy and makes a contrasting foil to the blooms. This variety is particularly good in the autumn when the yellow shading of the flowers is more prominent.

Pemberton, UK, 1913, continuous flowering 1.5 x 1.2 m (5 x 4 ft)

'Penelope'

Flowers are large and semi-double, with frilled petals of cream tinged soft pink, they open flat to reveal prominent golden stamens and are delightfully scented. Foliage is dark and growth upright. With regular dead-heading 'Penelope' will flower well into the autumn.

Pemberton, UK, 1924, continuous flowering, 1.5 x 1.2 m (5 x 4 ft)

Hybrid Perpetuals

The name of this group is a little misleading as they are not totally perpetual, although they will usually supply at least one second flush of flower each year. Most were bred in the early part of the 1800s and are the forerunners of the Hybrid Teas. The Victorians loved them for their big sumptuous blooms. Plants vary in size from tidy compact shrubs to those with more vigorous arching growth, but the flowers are nearly always scented, often powerfully. Best grown as companions to other roses or shrubs.

Above: 'Baronne Prévost' has large, very double strongly perfumed flowers.

'Baroness Rothschild'

This is a superior rose with very large, full and cupped flowers of clear rose pink with silky-textured petals. They are held erect on strong stems above abundant mid-green leaves. Growth is upright on a medium-sized shrub.
Pernet Père, France, 1868, repeat flowering, 1.2 x 1 m (4 x 3 ft)

'Baronne Prévost'

Very double blooms comprising many petals are strong rose pink and perfumed. They appear abundantly for the first flush of flowers but not quite as heavily later on. Growth can be a little willowy but bushy with dark leaves and many vicious thorns. An attractive rose that is best placed towards the back of the border.
Desprez, France, 1842, repeat flowering, 1.5 x 1.2 m (5 x 4 ft)

'Éclair'

Very dark red, almost black, velvety petals form fully double, very attractive and scented flowers. Growth is upright and prickly but can be a little sparse when it comes to foliage. A rose that grows best in well-nourished soil.
Lacharme, France, 1833, repeat flowering, 1.2 x 1 m (4 x 3 ft)

'Ferdinand Pichard'

Stripes of carmine stand out boldly against a pinky white background colour on the petals of double, well scented flowers. They appear repeatedly throughout summer on a vigorous shrub, which sends out long arms of new growth. Leaves are large and pointed.
Tanne, France, 1921, repeat flowering, 1.5 x 1.2 m (5 x 4 ft)

'Reine des Violettes'

Large double flowers are soft violet to lilac, ageing to a lilac grey, and have a lovely perfume. They are flat, quartered and petals furl in at the centre. Leaves are a grey green and stems are relatively smooth. This is an excellent garden rose and will even grow well in a tub.
Millet-Malet, France, 1860, continuous flowering, 1.5 x 1 m (5 x 3 ft)

Below: 'Ferdinand Pichard' is a focal point in any garden.

Modern Shrub roses and the new English roses

The Modern Shrub roses are a group consisting of roses of relatively recent introduction, called such because they are of mixed parentage, making them difficult to place elsewhere as there is no particular group with which any they have strong affinity. They are a diverse group with flowers in different colours, styles and sizes. Some are scented, some not very much. Most grow to above a metre and some can be adapted to climb in the right situation. The majority are relatively healthy, but there are some that need coddling to get the best from them and others that will withstand poor situations. This is, as you may imagine, a huge group so I have had to be very selective in choosing the varieties described below.

New English roses are also a group of mixed progeny, their name having been adopted for marketing purposes rather than for any other reason, but these days the word 'new' is generally dropped. In reality they are simply Modern Shrub roses. They are actually a combination of old roses, to which they owe their appearance, and new roses, Hybrid Teas and Floribundas mainly, which provide the 'English Roses' with their remontancy. Most of them are strong growing, with the occasional tendency to be a little lax and willowy; some are even suitable as small climbers. Although there are a few with an annoying tendency to pick up disease, most are healthy – but this is the case with all roses. Their use in the garden is varied; the shorter, bushier varieties are good in a tub or a shrubbery, which is the best place for larger specimens. They all seem to benefit from a good prune to keep them within bounds and to stop them becoming top heavy, and need regular dead-heading to perpetuate blooming.

'Cuthbert Grant'

The individual flowers are semi-double, deep velvety red with a proud circle of golden anthers, but it is more the combined effect of very many blooms that is stunning. A healthy rose with glossy leaves and vigorous growth. *Canadian Department of Agriculture, 1967, repeat flowering, 1.2 x 1 m (4 x 3 ft)*

Below: 'Henry Kelsey' is a healthy Modern Shrub rose.

'Graham Thomas'

This must rank as one of the best of the English Roses. Flowers are rich yellow, paling with age, cupped in shape, double and with a heady perfume. They appear in clusters on a willowy plant with dark to mid-green, glossy leaves.

English Rose, Austin, UK, 1983, continuous flowering, 1.2 x 1 m (4 x 3 ft)

'Jacqueline du Pré'

A super shrub rose with much to recommend it. Ivory cream blooms are semi-double in clusters with prominent pink to gold stamens; they are shaped very much like a water lily and have a musk-like perfume. Plump buds are buff to apricot. The foliage is dark and glossy.

Harkness, UK, 1989, repeat flowering, 1.2 x 1.5 m (4 x 5 ft)

'Lichtkönigin Lucia'

This is a very useful and healthy shrub rose. Semi-double flowers are bright yellow and scented, and appear in clusters. Growth is upright yet bushy with mid- to bright green, glossy foliage. There are few yellow shrub roses with the attributes of this one.

Kordes, Germany, 1966, continuous flowering, 1.2 x 1 m (4 x 3 ft)

Above: 'Macmillan Nurse' is very healthy and free flowering

'Macmillan Nurse'

The blooms that emerge from plump buds are very double, almost quartered, and white with a hint of peach at the base of the petals. They are borne in clusters on a healthy, strong-growing plant with dark glossy leaves and well-armed branches. As one bloom falls so another appears, all summer long.

Beales, UK, 1998, continuous flowering, 1 x 1 m (3 x 3 ft)

'Mary Rose'

Rich rose pink, scented blooms are old fashioned in style, being slightly cupped and very double, deeper pink at the centre. They are borne in clusters on the end of long and arching shoots. Foliage is glossy and dark, and growth dense and open in habit.

English Rose, Austin, UK, 1983, continuous flowering, 1.2 x 1 m (4 x 3 ft)

'Raymond Carver'

An excellent rose bred by Colin Horner but introduced to the marketplace by my father. Blooms are amber to apricot with buff undertones. They are very double, almost crinkled and are delightfully scented in clusters on the end of strong, straight stems. Leaves are large, dark and, when young, copper tinged. Will tolerate poor soils.

Beales, UK, 1999, continuous flowering, 1.2 x 1 m (4 x 3 ft)

'Sadler's Wells'

This variety is outstanding in the autumn when many other roses have finished blooming; it is good earlier on as well. Flowers are semi-double, silvery pink and heavily edged with cherry red. They appear in clusters of around five or six blooms on the end of long, strong and upright shoots. Leaves are dark and glossy. A good rose for cutting.

Beales, UK, 1983, continuous flowering, 1.2 x 1 m (4 x 3 ft)

'Westerland'

Although a little bright for my taste, this is a good all-rounder. Blooms are apricot to orange, large and a little shaggy with some scent, and they appear regularly throughout the summer. It is very vigorous and upright in habit with large mid- to dark green leaves. Tolerant of poorer situations.

Kordes, Germany, 1969, continuous flowering, 1.2 x 1 m (4 x 3 ft)

Moss roses

This is a fascinating family of roses, for it is perhaps not the flowers that are the most appealing features but the stems and unopened buds. They are endowed with moss-like glands – some varieties more than others – which, when touched, have a wonderful balsam-like fragrance. These roses are separately classified as Moss roses but this group really belongs to the Centifolias. It was a sport of *Rosa centifolia* called *R. centifolia muscosa* that first appeared early in the 19th century and was used extensively in breeding programmes, through which new varieties with moss-like glands were created. Some have masses of soft moss and there are some with many high-density thorns. I am sure that if they were not so novel there would be many in this group that would have become extinct, but every rose has its place and among the ranks of the Moss roses are some excellent varieties.

Above: 'Raymond Carver' cannot be beaten for its quantity of blooms and healthy disposition

'Alfred de Dalmas'

Although possibly related to the Portland Damasks, this rose warrants inclusion in this group because of its mossed stems. Blooms are semi-double, shell pink, cupped and scented. Unusually for a Moss, they appear reasonably continuously throughout the summer on a tidy plant with plentiful foliage. A good rose with several uses in the garden, not least of which is its suitability for growing in a tub.

Portemer, France, 1855, continuous flowering, 1 m x 60 cm (3 ft x 24 in)

'Chapeau de Napoléon'

The full, double highly scented flowers of this rose are delightful but not the reason for its popularity. The flower buds are heavily endowed with moss to the extent that they form a shape similar to that of a cocked hat. The resemblance is uncanny. Whatever its novelty value, this is a good shrub worthy of inclusion in the garden, although it can be a little lax in habit.

Vibert, France, 1826, summer flowering, 1.5 x 1.2 m (5 x 4 ft)

Above: 'Alfred de Dalmas' is the only Moss rose to produce more than one flush of flowers.

'Common Moss'

Also known as 'Old Pink Moss'. Probably a version of *Rosa centifolia muscosa*, of which it seems there are several. Flowers are mid-rose pink, double and highly perfumed. Well mossed with ample, slightly crinkled foliage. A good Moss rose which is perhaps most at home towards the back of the border.

France, before 1700, summer flowering, 1.2 x 1.2 m (4 x 4 ft)

'Nuits de Young'

Smallish flowers are purple to deep red, a colour which is intensified by contrasting golden anthers. Leaves are not large and moss is not overwhelming, but the colour of the flowers is eyecatching, a good focal point in among roses of other shades.

Laffay, France, 1845, summer flowering, 1.2 x 1 m (4 x 3 ft)

'William Lobb'

A very vigorous variety with long, arching canes of new growth. Flowers are borne in clusters and are a mixture of purple, lilac and grey, sometimes with a hint of pink. They are double and lightly scented. Can be grown as a small climber but may require some support even when encouraged to grow as a shrub.

Laffay, France, 1855, summer flowering, 2.5 x 1.5 m (8 x 5 ft)

Left: Like most of the Moss roses, 'Common Moss' has balsam-scented moss-like glands around the flower buds.

Pimpinellifolias or Scotch Briars

Also known as Burnets, this little group of very hardy roses is native to Europe. In form they are very prickly, compact and their foliage consists of many tiny serrated leaflets. The flowers are generally small, appearing in abundance in early summer and usually followed by a display of shiny, rotund, mahogany-coloured hips later in the year. They will grow almost anywhere, in a cool, shaded aspect or poor soil, and will cope with the worst winters, hence the name 'Scotch Briars'. A Robert Brown, of Perth Scotland, found a Scotch rose growing wild in the hills near Perth. He gathered the seed and it was sown at the nursery of Dickson & Brown in Perth in 1793. The seeds produced a double rose and, in time, variations of it were grown. The numbers of these little roses increased until, it is said, another Scottish grower had more than 100 varieties. English growers soon became aware of them and their popularity spread. Today many of these are lost, but we still have a good selection and many newer hybrids from which to choose. Their density and thorny disposition make them ideal candidates for the shorter boundary hedge, where sharp thorns will provide a good deterrent.

'Burnet Double White'

Flowers are cupped, semi-double and dainty with bright golden anthers. They are produced abundantly on small shrubs with masses of tiny serrated leaves. In the autumn the flowers are replaced by small round, dark and polished mahogany, almost black, hips. There are also pink and marbled pink versions named respectively 'Burnet Double Pink' and 'Burnet Marbled Pink'.

Of uncertain origin, likely to be before 1650, early summer/spring flowering 1 x 1 m (3 x 3 ft)

Above: 'Maigold' has many nasty prickles but is a useful healthy climber.

'Frühlingsduft'

There are a number of 'Frühlings' hybrids, all remarkably hardy and all bred by Kordes of Germany, but this has to be my favourite of them all. Flowers are fully double, creamy yellow with buff to pink tinges at their centres. Foliage is tough, slightly crinkled, glossy and dark green. A good rose but it does require space.

Kordes, Germany, 1949, summer flowering, 3 x 1.8 m (10 x 6 ft)

'Maigold'

A hybrid Pimpinellifolia that is best grown as a climber, although it will grow in the shrubbery if given some support. Blooms are semi-double apricot orange blending towards yellow at the centre. They are to my taste, bright but not gaudy, and have a superb cupped shape. Borne in clusters early in the year, with the odd repeating bloom, they sit amid the most healthy dark green glossy foliage. If there is a drawback to this variety it is the huge number of nasty thorns it possesses.

Kordes, Germany, 1953, early summer/spring flowering, 3.8 x 2.5 m (12 x 8 ft)

'Mary Queen of Scots'

An early-flowering variety that leaves you craving for further summer blooms. Flowers are single, creamy pink tinged deeper lilac pink, with prominent stamens. Leaves are tiny and there are masses of them on plum- to mahogany-coloured wood. Round hips follow the flowers and are deep maroon, almost black. A beautiful rose even if its blooms are short lived.

Of uncertain origin, very old, early summer/spring flowering, 1 x 1 m (3 x 3 ft)

Polyanthas

These little roses were very popular in the early 20th century; they are small-flowered, low-growing roses with many uses. Their habit allows them to be grown easily in pots on the patio or balcony and they also make good edging to beds and borders, as well as being free flowering and sufficiently low growing for bedding. The flowers tend to be small, in clusters, and appear freely over a long period. Regular dead-heading is important to extend the flowering period. Many of the Polyanthas have sported from others and it is not uncommon to find a stem that has reverted to the parent plant. The Polyanthas are often listed with Floribundas, but their growth habit is somewhat different: they tend to be shorter, a little more prostrate and produce larger trusses of smaller flowers.

'Baby Faurax'

The distinct violet colouring of the flowers of this little rose means that it stands out among other roses in this group. The flowers are double, cupped and held in large clusters, with streaks of white around prominent stamens. Growth is bushy, low and slightly spreading.

Lille, France, 1924, continuous flowering, 30 x 30 cm (12 x 12 in)

'Cameo'

Small flowers are held in large bunches. They are soft salmon to flesh pink, cupped in shape, revealing golden anthers when fully open. Growth is bushy and and well clothed with narrow, pointed, light green leaves.

de Ruiter, Holland, 1932, continuous flowering, 60 x 60 cm

(24 x 24 in)

Gloria Mundi

Large clusters of rich scarlet red flowers that are slightly cupped with white flecks at their centres. Growth is upright but bushy and clothed with many small dark leaves. Flowers freely into the autumn months but may occasionally throw out a stem that has reverted to the rose from which it sported.

de Ruiter, Holland, 1929, continuous flowering, 60 x 60 cm

(24 x 24 in)

'Miss Edith Cavell'

This little rose disappeared for quite a while but was reintroduced by my father on the 70th anniversary of the execution of Nurse Edith Cavell. At that time we lived in the village of her birth and it was only after an appeal in the local paper by the Vicar of Swardeston that the rose was found again. Small rich red to scarlet, double flowers are borne in large clusters. Small leaves are dark green and plentiful.

de Ruiter, Holland, 1917, continuous flowering, 60 x 60 cm

(24 x 24 in)

'The Fairy'

The branches of this attractive rose grow in an arching manner which make it a good subject for a pot, where they cascade outwards. The blooms are small, soft pink and bunched in large clusters. Leaves are mid- to deep green and glossy. 'The Fairy' benefits from regular removal of the dead flower clusters.

Bentall, UK, 1932, continuous flowering, 60 cm x 1.2 m

(24 in x 4 ft)

Above: 'The Fairy' has nodding clusters of bloom.

Portlands

Some of the most beautiful and easily managed old roses make up this small group. They are all at least repeat-flowering varieties and most give off expensive perfumes. They are neat and bushy in growth habit and are therefore an excellent choice for smaller gardens. Their tidy proportions allow them to grow well in pots, and they also make good low hedging and work well in formal group planting. Most of them will tolerate all but the very poorest of soil but they do not favour too much shade. Their colouring ranges from white, through soft and mid-pinks to deep purple reds.

'Arthur de Sansal'

The beautiful flowers are crimson purple, very double and rosette-like in formation. They are highly perfumed and appear repeatedly throughout the flowering season. A neat and bushy plant with large dark leaves. Unfortunately prone to mildew; probably not the best rose to include in an organic garden.

Cartier, France, 1847, repeat flowering, 1 m x 60 cm

(3 ft x 24 in)

Above: 'Comte de Chambord' is a useful smaller proportioned shrub.

'Comte de Chambord'

Large, very double flowers are rich glowing pink at the centre, where petals furl inwards, and softer pink towards the edge. They exude a strong and heady fragrance. Petals are delicate with a tissue-paper-like quality. The plant is not large but the leaves, which are bright to grey green, are big.

Moreau-Robert, France, 1863, continuous flowering, 1 m x 60 cm (3 ft x 24 in)

'Duchess of Portland'

Also known as 'Portland Rose' this was the first rose of its type. Borne in small clusters, the flowers are semi-double, cerise with prominent stamens. Only slightly fragrant, they appear repeatedly throughout the summer. Foliage is mid- to light green and the wood is prickly. Growth is tidy.

Introducer unknown, probably from Italy, around 1790, repeat flowering, 1 m x 60 cm (3 ft x 24 in)

'Jacques Cartier'

Flat blooms are soft mid-pink and highly scented. Petals towards the centre furl in, while those on the outer edges often furl away from the flower. The blooms are held erect on strong stems amid leathery mid-green foliage. In the USA 'Jacques Cartier' is sold under the name 'Marquise Boccella'.

Moreau-Robert, France, 1686, continuous flowering, 1 m x 60 cm (3 ft x 24 in)

Procumbents

'Ground cover' is a commonly used term in the garden but there are few roses that truly cover the ground. At our nursery, we prefer to call them Procumbent roses, which more readily describes their arching, wide-growing habit. There are many ways of growing them, from hiding eyesores such as manhole covers to spilling down banks or tumbling over walls, and some will even be happy in hanging baskets. In the right position, when against a wall for example, they can be encouraged to climb and the more vigorous of them will easily grow through the branches of established hedges, where they will provide added colour and increased density to the hedge. Most of the Procumbents have small flowers in a varied palette, some are perfumed and several of them set hips after flowering.

'Bonica '82'

This is an exceptional variety that seems never to be without a flower for the whole of the summer and well into the autumn. From tiny buds cupped, mid-rose pink flowers that are tight and cupped, these gradually open to form almost flat, slightly frilled, more faded blooms with insignificant anthers of a curious pinkish brown. They appear in clusters which invariably consist of flowers at many stages, from buds showing no sign of colour to spent blooms. Foliage is healthy and dark, and growth is bushy yet spreading.

Meilland, France, 1982, continuous flowering, 1 x 1.8 m (3 x 6 ft)

'Fairyland'

I am fond of this little rose, for while it does not possess the vigorous qualities of some of its counterparts, it is very pretty and I personally find it to be highly scented. Flowers in bunches are fully double, cupped in shape and soft pink fading to near-white with age. Foliage is dark and glossy and, provided it is regularly dead-headed, it will flower for a long period. Growth is dense and capable of producing good, if not instant coverage.

Harkness, UK, 1980, continuous flowering, 60 cm x 1.5 m (24 in x 5 ft)

'Grouse'

This can be a stunning rose in the right situation. While only producing scant repeat

Below: 'Grouse' is one of the most vigorous Procumbents and will happily scramble over banks and through hedges.

blooms, its first flush is magnificent and somewhat later than many other garden roses – useful to remember when you are at the planning stage. Flowers are single and white from soft pink to white buds; leaves are dark and glossy, very much like *Rosa wichuraiana*, which is in its blood. Growth is vigorous and capable of many tasks. We have a couple of plants at our nursery, planted in a bed against a beech hedge. They have covered the bed and fought their way through and over the hedge. When in full flush they fill the adjacent car park with the most lovely perfume. Tiny hips follow in the autumn.

Kordes, Germany, 1982, repeat flowering, 60 cm x 3 m (24 in x 10 ft)

'Macrantha Raubritter'

Although to be correct this rose should be listed among the *Rosa macrantha* hybrids, I have not divided this directory so finely as to give them a separate section; however, the habit of this rose warrants its inclusion here. Charming cupped semi-double flowers are mid- to soft rose pink in clusters. Branches are rather thorny and leaves generally grey green. Can be a little prone to mildew but this is a once-flowering rose and attacks usually occur after flowering.

Kordes, Germany, 1967, summer flowering, 1 x 1.8 m (3 x 6 ft)

'Summer Sunrise'

The result of a cross between 'Bonica '82' and 'New Dawn', this rose displays qualities that can be attributed to both parents. Semi-double blooms are small and soft to bright pink. They open flat to display lovely golden stamens. Leaves are dark and glossy on vigorous growth. 'Summer Sunrise' is a free-flowering rose that, if dead-headed regularly, will produce blooms well into the autumn.

Beales, UK, 1994, continuous flowering, 45 cm x 1 m (18 in x 3 ft)

Rugosas

Thorny, dense-growing plants with an upright habit, the Rugosas are perfect intruder deterrents when planted along a boundary. Flowers appear regularly throughout the summer and, in many varieties, are followed by splendid orange, tomato-shaped hips which are often of giant proportions. In accompaniment to the hips, the leaves will adopt various attractive hues in the autumn, from yellow through orange to umber, a combination that is stunningly beautiful. Rewarding even to the inexperienced gardener, in difficult conditions they make excellent sturdy hedges or are candidates for the mixed shrubbery.

Above: Rugosa roses are useful for hedging. Many of them will set impressive hips in the autumn.

'Agnes'

This is a hybrid of *Rosa rugosa* and *R. foetida persiana*, and owes its colouring to the latter of the two. Flowers are double, soft apricot-yellow, fading to near-white with age and set off by dark leaves that are smaller than those of most Rugosas. Stems are well armed with nasty prickles. Odd flowers appear after the first flush which, in a good season, can be a truly lovely sight.

Saunders Central Experimental Farm, Canada, 1922, repeat flowering, 1.8 x 1.5 m (6 x 5 ft)

'Belle Poitevine'

Due to crinkled petals, the flowers of this cultivar tend to have a rather unkempt appearance, which in many ways adds to their attractiveness. They are mid-silvery pink verging on lilac, scented and have a golden coronet of anthers at the centre. Leaves are bright green, heavily veined and healthy. A strong-growing plant that only occasionally sets hips.

Bruant, France 1894, repeat flowering 1.8 x 1.5 m (6 x 5 ft)

'Blanc Double de Coubert'

Large flat flowers are pure white, double and sweetly scented. This is an excellent, free-flowering Rugosa, setting hips intermittently, with strong rich green foliage and many needle-like thorns. Lovely autumn leaves. A good candidate for hedging.

Cochet-Cochet, France, 1892, repeat flowering, 1.5 x 1.2 m (5 x 4 ft)

'Roseraie de l'Hay'

A popular variety very often used in hedging. Blooms are large, semi-double crimson magenta opening flat and ragged, with a clove-like scent. Flowers appear often during the summer and into autumn. Growth is bushy and leaves bright green and heavily veined. Autumn colouring is stunning but it rarely sets hips.

Cochet-Cochet, France, 1901, continuous flowering, 1.8 x 1.5 m (6 x 5 ft)

'Scabrosa'

This rose is best known for its fruit, which are large, bright orange red and look like tomatoes. They are often seen on the plant at the same time as the flowers, which are large, single with almost wing-like petals of rich silvery pink. Sweetly scented, they are borne amid heavily veined rich green leaves on an upright, dense plant. Good autumn foliage.

Harkness, UK, 1960, continuous flowering, 1.8 x 1.2 m (6 x 4 ft)

Species

These are the predecessors of all modern-day hybrid roses; they are the wild or true roses of nature and, as such, although they vary widely, all possess a natural, simple and pure charm. The majority have single flowers, in varying shades but usually white or pink, followed by hips in different sizes, shapes and in varying degrees of orange to red, and even mahogany and black in the case of *Rosa pimpinellifolia*. They are healthy roses when compared to hybrid varieties and most are hardy.

While they have many similarities, the fact that these roses are unrelated to each other means that there are some very individual traits to be found. Some are early flowering, others produce blooms later on, but very few are repeat flowering; they can be large or small in growth, with different shades and shapes of leaves. I value these roses greatly, for not only are they important historically but also they are delightful in themselves. Interestingly, while these roses are individually attributed as species, there is often more than one clone of each. This is because they have altered in some way, often only very slightly, by natural genetic modification in adapting to wider distribution in the wild, such as climate and soil in new locations. In the larger garden they can show off their characteristics, and are well suited to the conservation garden, parks and woodland.

Rosa canina

Also known as the 'Dog Rose'. This is the wild rose commonly found growing in hedges the length and breadth of Britain and indeed in some European locations. Flowers are single, from blush pink to white and are borne along lengths of arching branches, well dressed in narrow grey green leaves and heavily armed with thorns. Bright red hips follow in the autumn.
Europe, before 1730, summer flowering, 1.8 x 3 m (6 x 10 ft)

Above: *Rosa glauca* has wonderful, pewter grey foliage.

Rosa foetida

This is a charming, brightly coloured rose. Single flowers are bright yellow with brown stamens. Young branches are tinged with plum and have long spiteful thorns. Leaves are soft mid-grey green and make up well-populated leaflets. As the name suggests, the fragrance of this rose is not good. Closely related to it are *Rosa foetida* bicolour, which is bright orange red, and *R. foetida persiana*, a double yellow that is largely responsible for the yellow colouring found in many modern roses and also sadly for their proneness to black spot.
Asia Minor, before 1600, summer flowering, 2.5 x 1.5 m (8 x 5 ft)

Rosa glauca

Also known as *Rosa rubrifolia* and possibly one of the best known species roses. Thornless stems are purple to red and are beautifully clothed with the main attraction of this rose, its delightful pewter grey leaves. The flowers are individually insignificant, even *en masse* they inspire little delight, but in the autumn the hips that replace them do. Drooping bunches of them are rather like cherries and they are set off by lovely autumn colouring of the leaves.
Europe, 1830, summer flowering, 1.8 x 1.5 m (6 x 5 ft)

Rosa sericea pteracantha

The appeal of this rose does not come from the flowers but from the huge thorns that, without break, adorn the whole lengths of the arching branches. In shape they are wedge-like, tapering off to nasty hooked points. On young growth they are translucent with the sun behind them, a glowing shade of mahogany red. The only significance of the flowers is the fact that they have only four petals, a feature found in this species only. Leaves are small and fern-like. There are one or two other closely related sericea species and only a few hybrids.

China, pre-1890, early summer flowering, 3 x 1.8 m (10 x 6 ft)

Rosa virginiana

Reddish brown stems produce only a few thorns. The leaves, which are bright green during the summer months, develop shades of amber and yellow changing to russet in the autumn, accompanied by polished red rotund hips. The flowers are beautiful, soft pink, sometimes dappled with a deeper shade; they are single and have beautiful prominent, dusty stamens.

North America, around 1807, summer flowering, 1.5 x 1 m (5 x 3 ft)

Below: *Rosa sericea pteracantha* has only four petals in each flower and stunning thorns.

Sweet Briars or Eglanterias

These roses, with the odd exception, have deliciously apple-scented foliage that is strongest from young succulent shoots and leaves. It is best appreciated when the leaves are gently squeezed but it will pervade the air after rain, on damp dewy mornings and during balmy summers evenings. The collection we have available to us now is undoubtedly smaller than it was, for several have been lost over the years. Most of them will bear just one flush of flowers followed by hips in the autumn, but there are one or two repeat-flowering Sweet Briars; however, these are hybrids and tend not to have aromatic foliage. It is wise to cut back the Sweet Briars to some extent to encourage the young growth that emits the most fragrance. These roses are perfect in natural settings, in wild or conservation areas, but are also suited to the garden, where they are best in a mixed setting of other roses, shrubs and perennials.

'Amy Robsart'

Blooms are semi-double, bright but deep glowing pink with white at their centres where they have a coronet of yellow stamens. When in full flush this rose is spectacular. Leaves are not overly perfumed but they are tough and clothe vigorous arching, slightly angular branches. A hardy variety tolerant of shade and poor soil.

Penzance, UK, 1890s, summer flowering, 3 x 2.5 m (10 x 8 ft)

'Lady Penzance'

The foliage of this lovely rose is among the most highly scented in this little group and is tough and leathery. Pretty flowers are single, copper to salmon with hints of pink, changing to yellow at their centres with bold yellow stamens. Bright red hips follow the flowers in the autumn. A strong-growing variety, tolerant of most situations.

Penzance, UK, 1890s, summer flowering, 2.1 x 1.8 m (7 x 6 ft)

Above: 'Lord Penzance' has apple-scented leaves.

'Lord Penzance'

This gentleman was responsible for several Sweet Briars in the latter years of the 19th century. Flowers are soft buff yellow with a suggestion of pink and has pronounced golden stamens. This variety hips well in the autumn and, along with 'Lady Penzance', has nicely scented foliage.

Penzance, UK, 1890s, summer flowering 2.1 x 1.8 m (7 x 6 ft)

'Meg Merrilies'

An excellent variety with crimson red, semi-double blooms in profusion in midsummer; the colouring of the petals is a contrast to the bright yellow stamens found within them. Both flowers and leaves are scented. A strong-growing, tough variety that is well armed with thorns. Hips well later in the year.

Penzance, UK, 1890s, summer flowering, 2.5 x 2.1 m (8 x 7 ft)

Teas

These are not the hardiest of roses but there are some delightfully beautiful, heavily perfumed varieties. In colder climates it is a good idea to grow them in pots so that they can be over wintered in a cool greenhouse or conservatory, otherwise they will require some protection in winter. It is difficult to fault them with anything other than their tenderness, except that some produce blooms of such size that they cause the fragile branches to bow

under their weight. They originated in the Far East where Sir Abraham Hume discovered *Rosa indica odorata*, now more frequently known as 'Hume's Blush', in 1810. It is thought that this rose, along with a few other Teas, was transported to Europe aboard ships of the East India Company carrying tea, hence their name, while others suggest that the name is a comparison to their perfume, but not according to my nose.

'Archiduc Joseph'

The muddled, flat flowers of this wonderful rose are made up from a palette including pink, copper, apricot and purple with hints of yellow here and there; this combination may sound awful but the effect is most lovely. One of the hardier Teas, with purple-tinted young growth and leaves and very few thorns. Placed against a wall it can be grown as a small climber.

G. Nabonnand, France, 1872, continuous flowering, 1.5 x 1 m (5 x 3 ft)

Below: 'Archiduc Joseph' has many different colours in its intricate flowers.

'Clementina Carbonieri'

The colouring of the flowers on this delightful rose is similar in all respects to 'Archiduc Joseph' except it is more muted. They are scented and a little shaggy, almost quartered in style. Foliage is dark and glossy on a bushy plant that is ideal in a pot, placed in a good location in the garden.

Bonfiglioli, Italy, 1913, continuous flowering, 1 m x 60 cm (3 ft x 24 in)

'Lady Hillingdon'

The apricot blooms of this superb rose start out from a long pointed bud opening shaggy and loose, and they exude a fantastic perfume. Young leaves and shoots are deep plum purple, a contrasting foil for the blooms. Growth is not hardy but this rose will get through most winters even if damaged by the frost. A climbing form is also available.

Lowe and Shawyer, UK, 1910, continuous flowering, 1 m x 60 cm (3 ft x 24 in)

'Mme Bravy'

This is an old Tea rose and a very beautiful one too. Double flowers are large and blowsy, creamy white tinged blush with a strong perfume, which is said by some to be reminiscent of tea and, by others, of raspberries. They appear in abundance on a dense, well-foliated bush that is ideal in size for growing in a container.

Guillot Père, France, 1846, continuous flowering 1 m x 60 cm (3 ft x 24 in)

'Tipsy Imperial Concubine'

Discovered in China by Mrs Hazel le Rougetel, this is thought to be an old Chinese cultivar. Large globular flowers are soft pink, overlaid with shades of yellow and sometimes tinged red. It is scented and very free flowering. Growth bushy.

Beales, UK, 1982, continuous flowering, 60 x 60 cm (24 x 24 in)

Climbing and rambling roses

When it comes to roses, one of the questions I am most frequently asked is, what is the difference between a climber and a rambler? To give a simple answer, one could say that climbers climb and ramblers ramble, which is a useful rule of thumb when selecting varieties and is probably the most relevant factor when deciding which rose is most suitable for a specific purpose. It is also generally true that ramblers are more vigorous, but these are only generalizations and there are more precise differences than these.

Climbers flower on growth they have produced earlier in the same season but ramblers only flower on the growth they have made in the previous season, which is why pruning methods are different for each of these groups.

Many climbers flower repeatedly or continuously throughout the summer months, while ramblers usually have just one flush – this is often followed by hips in the autumn. Generally speaking, since ramblers are more vigorous than climbers, they will cope with more demanding duties such as growing through the branches of trees or over unsightly buildings, for example, while climbers are happier when growing on pillars, or against trellis or walls.

With both climbers and ramblers, it will probably take two or three years before they begin to look established and often this long before the very vigorous ramblers will start to flower at all. It is also interesting to note that some of the most vigorous Procumbent (ground cover) roses will perform very well as ramblers and, conversely, if they are left to tumble, many ramblers will, given time, cover the ground.

Climbers

Above: 'Blairii Number Two' is one of the most beautiful of the climbing Bourbons.

Climbing Bourbons

This is just a small group but it numbers within its ranks some of the loveliest climbing roses of all. It is true that some of the shrub Bourbons can be grown as small climbers with support, but the ones I have included here are much more vigorous than those. Most flower abundantly, a few over a long season, but their best attraction must be the perfume they exude. If a fault can be found at all with these roses it is their tendency to mildew later in the season. To avoid this or at least keep the attack of mildew to a minimum, try to plant these roses in open, airy positions and avoid very dry spots.

'Blairii Number Two'

This is a truly magnificent variety when in full flower, and although any later blooming, will not obliterate the foliage in the way that the first does, the flowers are still delightful. The large blooms are double pale pink deepening towards the centre and they are very fragrant. Foliage is mid-green and shiny.

Blair, UK, 1845, repeat flowering, 3.8 x 1.8 m (12 x 6 ft)

'Souvenir de la Malmaison, Climbing'

Like its bushy counterpart, this variety has the most beautiful flat and quartered blooms of soft powder pink to ivory. They are exquisitely perfumed but do hate wet weather, when they easily become balled. The remedy for this is to tease open the outer damaged petals, allowing those within to develop properly; this must be done in haste though, before the base of all the petals decays.

Bennett, UK, 1893, repeat flowering 3.8 x 2.5 m (12 x 8 ft)

'Zéphirine Drouhin'

This rose has much sentimental value for me, for a bloom of it was laid on the font for my christening, my father had flowers of it imported for my wedding and, in turn, I had a bloom of it present at the christening of my daughter. 'Zéphirine Drouhin' has two or three splendid qualities: it is thornless, highly perfumed and capable of flowering well into the autumn. Flowers are deep cerise pink, semi-double and a little muddled.

Bizot, France, 1868, continuous flowering, 3 x 1.8 m (10 x 6 ft)

Boursaults

This is a group like no other and there is no positive evidence to suggest from which roses they originally descended. While they mostly flower only once on growth from the previous season, I include them here with other climbers as their growth habit cannot in any way be described as rambling. They are all thornless and share the attributes of arching smooth stems and long pointed foliage. Blooms, too, bear similarities to each other, being generally rather unkempt and in the more double forms almost quartered. In colouring they are all similar, ranging from mid-pink to pinkish red.

Above: 'Mme Grégoire Staechelin' is one of the first roses to bloom each year.

'Amadis'

Also known as 'Crimson Boursault'. The semi-double medium-sized flowers of crimson purple are slightly cupped and a little unkempt when fully open. They can be found borne singly or in small clusters. Mature wood is plum coloured. At its happiest it may produce the odd repeat bloom but it is generally summer flowering only.

France, 1829, summer flowering, 3 x 1.8 m (10 x 6 ft)

'Blush Boursault'

Beautiful flowers are pale, blush pink and double. Growth is less purple than some but still heavily coloured and leaves are a dark, matt green. This is a more vigorous member of the Boursault group.

France, 1848, summer flowering, 4.5 x 3 m (15 x 10 ft)

'Mme Sancy de Parabère'

Mid- to soft pink petals are laid out in an almost quartered style, with those outermost usually slightly softer than those in the centre. Leaves are dark and characteristically thin and pointed, and wood is more brown than purple on mature plants.

France, mid-1870s, summer flowering 4.5 x 3 m (15 x 10 ft)

'Morlettii'

Double flowers are magenta to pink, with petals furling inwards quite tightly at the centre of the flower but more loosely displayed around at the edges. As it is less vigorous than the other Boursaults, 'Morlettii' can make a useful free-standing shrub rose, especially with the benefit of some support.

France, 1880s, summer flowering, 2.5 x 1.8 m (8 x 6 ft)

Climbing Hybrid Teas

The climbing Hybrid Teas are the result of a bush Hybrid Tea, suddenly and without any apparent reason, sending out a long, arching, climbing branch. As with all things unexpected, the perpetuation of the climbing capabilities of these roses came about only by chance: a knowledgeable nurseryman must have realized that what was before him was more than a gangly branch and had material from it taken for propagation rather than simply pruning it back, as many gardeners would do. Thanks to their wits we now have a race of excellent climbing roses. While their bush counterparts flower more or less continuously, the climbers

Plant directory

found here have a mad flush with a repeat blooming in late summer to early autumn. They excel as climbers but need training and pruning to stop them becoming top heavy.

'Château de Clos Vougeot'

The blooms are double and deep red, handing out an expensive perfume; the texture of the petals can only be compared to velvet. Like many climbing Hybrid Teas, the dark foliage is fairly spaced out, revealing strong, relatively thornless stems. A vigorous if somewhat angular growing variety.

Morse, UK, 1920, summer flowering, 5.4 x 2.5 m (15 x 8 ft)

'Cupid'

Blooms are large, single, soft flesh to powder pink, nearing primrose at the centre with golden anthers. A mature plant will produce many blooms at once but very few if any later on. Growth can be angular with sparse foliage, but this is not a problem if it can be grown intermingled with a better clothed plant. Large plump hips of pale orange, follow the flowers. A good rose well worth space in the garden.

B.R. Cant, UK, 1915, summer flowering, 3 x 1.8 m (10 x 6 ft)

Below: 'Mme Sancy de Parabère' has ragged flowers.

'Étoile de Hollande, Climbing'

Perhaps the biggest fault of the bush form of this rose is that it hangs its head, preventing the onlooker from fully appreciating its glory. This is perhaps the best point about the climbing form: those looking at the blooms can enjoy their perfection as they nod down towards them. Fully double, these nodding flowers are deep velvety red and share with those partaking a wonderful perfume. With age the red turns to purple, especially in full sun. Leaves are deep green and young growth tinged beetroot.

Leenders, Holland, 1931, summer flowering, 3.8 x 2.5 m (12 x 8 ft)

'Mme Caroline Testout, Climbing'

The flowers of this rose are like miniature cabbages, although rose pink as opposed to green. They really are fully double to the extent that they are globular with the tips of the outer petals reflexing until they are fully open. The perfume they emit is wonderful. As with most roses in this group, the leaves are well spaced and growth can be angular, but this is easily overcome with training. A good rose that will produce the odd second bloom.

Ketten Bros, Luxembourg, 1921, repeat flowering, 3.8 x 2.5 m (12 x 8 ft)

'Mme Grégoire Staechelin'

One of the most inspiring garden roses as it is one of the first double-flowered, highly scented varieties to bloom each year, giving a promise of all those to follow. Loosely double, large almost bell-like flowers are soft pink, a little deeper on the outside, and appear in profusion in late spring to early summer, with the odd repeating bloom later on. Foliage is a little coarse but growth is reasonably vigorous. Huge hips appear later on if the plant is not dead headed.

Dot, Spain, 1927, repeat flowering, 4.5 x 3 m (15 x 10 ft)

Climbing Floribundas

As with the climbing Hybrid Teas, climbing Floribundas are the result of the bush version of the variety having produced a sport, in other words developing a shoot with climbing capabilities. Propagation material taken from this branch resulted in plants with total climbing capabilities. The flowers of the climbing form are in all respects identical to the bush form but they usually only appear in one abundant flush, while their shorter growing kin will flower pretty well non-stop during the summer and into the autumn. There are not many commercially available but those that are can be useful additions to the garden.

'Allgold, Climbing'

'Allgold' is well known for its strong yellow, unfading blooms so is a useful climber when a bright colour is needed. They are semi-double, of average size, lightly perfumed and are set off by dark and glossy foliage. The clusters, or occasional single flowers, are held erect on strong stems. A good all-round climber.

Gandy, UK, 1961, summer flowering, 4.5 x 3 m (15 x 10 ft)

Below: The climbing version of 'Allgold' is a sport of the bush form.

'Iceberg, Climbing'

Iceberg is a famous rose and the climbing form deserves similar recognition. Flowers emerge from cream buds, opening pure white and semi-double in small clusters. Sadly not fragrant but certainly abundant. Leaves are no more than mid-green, sometimes pale green, but the contrast with the white may make them seem darker. A climber of reasonable vigour with flexible growth that is easily trained.

Cants, UK, 1968, summer flowering, 5 x 3 m (18 x 10 ft)

'Masquerade, Climbing'

Perhaps not my favourite variety but useful when bright shocking colour is needed. Semi-double blooms open yellow and change as they mature through shades of orange and pink to red; they are borne in clusters. Stems are thorny and vigorous and clothed in dark, fairly healthy foliage.

Gregory, UK, 1958, summer flowering, 5 x 3 m (18 x 10 ft)

'Queen Elizabeth, Climbing'

The bush form of 'Queen Elizabeth' is one of the most vigorous Floribundas, so it stands to reason that the climbing form is capable of reaching great heights. Blooms are large, silvery pink in clusters and are moderately fragrant. Leaves too are large and leathery. This variety needs careful pruning and training to prevent it from becoming top heavy.

Wheatcroft, UK, 1960, summer flowering, 6 x 3 m (20 x 10 ft)

Modern Climbers

In common with the Modern Shrub roses, these climbers have such diverse parentage that they do not fall into any other specific classification, therefore in order to give them a title they are grouped together under this heading. Among their ranks are some excellent roses of varying characteristics, from hugely vigorous to shorter growing varieties. There is a

Above: 'Aloha' is best used as a pillar rose.

Modern Climber available in any natural rose colour, some are highly perfumed, some not much. I probably need not go on. This is a large group of roses and it is impossible to include them all here, so I have selected a range with various colours and styles.

'Aloha'

Not the most vigorous climber, in fact probably better described as a pillar rose. The blooms are very double, deep rose pink with the occasional hint of salmon and magenta; they are superbly perfumed. Foliage is dark and glossy on an upright plant that is seldom without flower.

Boerner, USA, 1949, continuous flowering, 3 x 1.8 m (10 x 6 ft)

'City of York'

I grow to love this rose more each time I see it. The semi-double flowers open cupped from creamy yellow buds, then become creamy white with hints of lemon at the centre where they display a crown of golden stamens. They are lightly perfumed and are produced freely and abundantly, often giving a second flush in autumn. Foliage is dark and glossy and growth pliable; an easy rose to train.

Tantau, Germany, 1960, summer flowering, 4.5 x 3 m (15 x 10 ft)

'Dublin Bay'

Double flowers of average proportions are deep, unfading, blood red, cupped in shape and quite beautiful. They are borne in small clusters continuously throughout the summer and well into the autumn. Foliage is healthy mid-green and very glossy. Its upright habit allows it to be grown as a large shrub, otherwise it is best on a pillar.

McGredy, UK, 1976, continuous flowering, 2.1 x 1.5 m (7 x 5 ft)

'Eden Rose '88'

A shorter growing climber in the old-fashioned style. The large flowers are very double, almost a perfect ball until they are fully open, creamy white to blush blending with deeper pink edging to the petals. They are borne in small clusters against dark foliage.

Meilland, France, 1987, continuous flowering , 2.5 x 1.8 m (8 x 6 ft)

'Golden Showers'

This is a well-known climber of average size. Large blooms are semi-double, shaggy, deep golden yellow at first, fading as they mature to a creamy yellow and displaying dark contrasting anthers. Leaves are dark and glossy, a superb foil to the flowers, and growth is upright and a little bushy. Flowers well into the autumn.

Lammerts, USA, 1956, continuous flowering, 3 x 1.8 m (10 x 6 ft)

'Leverkusen'

A superb and healthy yellow climber. Lemon yellow flowers are double, rosette-like in shape, sweetly scented with crinkled petals. They appear continuously, with the odd break throughout the summer, against dark, leathery, deeply veined foliage. Growth is vigorous, slender and easy to tie in. This climber will grow well in almost any aspect and will cope with poor soils.

Kordes, Germany, 1954, continuous flowering, 3 x 2.5 m (10 x 8 ft)

'Swan Lake'

The flowers of this variety are at their most beautiful when the petals first begin to unfurl. They are white with flesh pink tones and deeper pink shades at the base maturing to near pure white, and are freely produced in small clusters. Foliage is dark and growth upright and tidy. A good pillar rose.

McGredy, UK, 1968, continuous flowering, 2.5 x 1.8 m (8 x 6 ft)

Noisettes

The Noisettes are among the most beautiful climbing roses of all, in my opinion. They are refined roses, in soft shades of pink, white and yellow in particular, not at all garish, just

Above: 'Parkdirektor Riggers' has glossy leaves.

perfectly natural. There are vigorous varieties and those which are rather less so, one or two very hardy ones and a few that may need careful siting to protect them from the worst of the winter weather. They are relatively easy to grow in the garden and, although some may have a susceptibility to mildew later in the season, they are generally healthy.

'Alister Stella Gray'

Borne in clusters, the slightly muddled flowers which consist of small, almost folded petals are soft yellow with deeper centres. They are flat and scented. Foliage is dark and growth slender and relatively thornless. The first flush of flowers is always the best but you do occasionally get further odd blooms later on.

A. H. Gray, UK 1894, repeat flowering, 4.5 x 3 m (15 x 10 ft)

'Blush Noisette'

An excellent little rose of accommodating proportions that can be grown as a large shrub if given support. Not vigorous, so patience will be needed when wanting it to climb. From deep pink, tubby buds emerge small flowers in large clusters. They are soft pink, with tints of lilac, fading with age. Leaves are dark green on dark wood that carries few thorns.

Noisette, USA, 1825, continuous flowering , 2.1 x 1.2 m (7 x 4 ft)

'Céline Forestier'

The blooms of this variety are larger than those of 'Alister Stella Gray' with more petals, and are a more intense yellow with a faint tinge of pink. They open flat with infurled centre petals. A free-

Below: 'Mme Alfred Carrière'will cope with poor situations.

Above: 'Céline Forestier' is a beautiful, scented climbing rose.

flowering variety that flowers late into the season. Growth is pliable and foliage a light green. A smaller climber that is happy grown in a pot.

Trouillard, France, 1842, continuous flowering, 2.5 x 1.2 m (8 x 4 ft)

'Desprez à Fleurs Jaune'

Flowers are smaller than many in this group; cascading in clusters, they are a delicate buff to pink shade, opening loose and blowsy. They exude a fresh fruity perfume. This is a vigorous Noisette which is easily trained. It is tolerant of shade and poor soil, and makes a good tree climber.

Desprez, France, 1835, repeat flowering, 6 x 3 m (20 x 10 ft)

'Mme Alfred Carrière'

Given that this rose is over a century old it is still very popular today, not only because it will grow well on a cool wall and in shade, but because it is also exquisitely beautiful. Shaggy, double blooms are creamy white with the odd tinge of pink and are heavily perfumed. Leaves are light to mid-green and growth is slender and relatively thorn free.

J. Schwartz, France, 1879, continuous flowering, 4.5 x 3 m (15 x 10 ft)

Climbing Teas

The Climbing Tea roses need careful placing in positions that will protect them against the worst of the winter weather, as they are not very hardy. If this is possible in your garden, they will repay you handsomely with beautiful flowers and fantastic perfume. This is not a large group of roses and sadly many have been lost over the years, probably because of their tenderness and delicacy.

'Adam'

The beautiful, heavily scented blooms of this rose are large, double and best described as buff to apricot with an overlay of pink. When open they are almost quartered. Ample leaves are dark and large and growth is not vigorous. It can be grown as a large shrub in the right situation and is happy in a pot.

Adam, UK, 1833, repeat flowering , 2.1 x 1.5 m (7 x 5 ft)

'Gloire de Dijon'

This is a favourite climber with large, quartered flowers of buff apricot with tinges of salmon towards the base of the petals. It has a very strong, heady perfume. Growth is vigorous with young shoots tinged with bronze. Other leaves are dark green and plentiful. Although this is one of the most beautiful roses, it hates wet weather, when the flowers become balled as the outer petals stick together. The only remedy for this is to carefully tease them away so that the remaining petals may unfurl.

Jacotot, France, 1853, repeat flowering, 3.8 x 2.5 m (12 x 8 ft)

'Sombreuil'

This is one of my favourites. Large white rosette-shaped flowers open flat from fat buds of cream. They are chiefly white with pinky apricot at the base of the petals. The perfume they emit is outstanding. Growth is vigorous and easily trained, leaves dark and on the whole healthy. Flowers freely often with a second flush.

Robert, France, 1843, repeat flowering, 3 x 2.5 m (10 x 8 ft)

'Souvenir de Mme Léonie Viennot, Climbing'

This is a lovely rose which was reintroduced by my father to the UK; he had been given budwood from a friend whose mother had sent it, wrapped in polythene in a pencil case, from New Zealand. Individual flowers are not huge, soft yellow heavily tinged with salmon, and the overall effect is charming. They are fragrant on a fairly vigorous plant with dark green leaves.

Bernaix, France, 1897, repeat flowering, 3.8 x 2.5 m (12 x 8 ft)

Ramblers
Arvensis hybrids

Having derived from our native Field Rose, this group (also known as Ayrshires) share its hardiness and naturally dignified simplicity. They serve many purposes, for their growth habits make them well suited to scrambling across the ground, intermingling with other ramblers and reaching some quite considerable heights in the garden. On the whole they are quite thorny and share a tendency to dark plum-coloured new growth.

'Venusta Pendula'

An ancient variety which was reintroduced to the market in the early 1900s. Pink buds open to reveal double white, flushed pink clusters of unscented small flowers. Growth can be twiggy but young shoots are delightfully deep plum maroon and foliage is also dark, a lovely foil for the blooms. A reasonably vigorous variety.

Kordes, Germany, 1928, summer flowering, 5 x 3 m (18 x 10 ft)

Right: 'Sombreuil' is a versatile, very free-flowering and heavily scented climber.

'Janet B. Wood'

This variety was rediscovered in by a Mrs McQueen of Ayrshire, Scotland, and reintroduced by my father. Small flowers are double, white and held in clusters on a strong-growing plant with dark plentiful foliage and wood that is also dark in colour. It is believed to be the original double Ayrshire rose first introduced in 1768. It will cope with all situations from poor soil and shade to a cool, dark aspect and is relatively vigorous.

Originally introduced in 1768, reintroduced by Beales, UK, 1984, summer flowering, 4.5 x 3 m (15 x 10 ft)

'Dundee Rambler'

This charming rose was bred in Scotland around the year 1850. I find the double, infurled white-tinged pink blooms quite delightful; they are borne in large nodding clusters set off by splendid dark leaves. Growth is dense, vigorous and thorny on a hardy plant with the capability of covering many an eyesore, such as a tumbledown shed or dead tree.

Martin, Scotland, around 1850, summer flowering, 6 x 3 m (20 x 10 ft)

Above: *Rosa arvensis* is a native of Europe commonly called The Field Rose.

Below: 'Dundee Rambler' is very hardy.

Moschata ramblers

Also referred to as the Musk ramblers, this small group includes some beautiful roses. Those I describe below are closely related to *Rosa moschata* but there are many more varieties with moschata blood somewhere in their history.

'Paul's Himalayan Musk'

This must be one of the best known, small-flowered pink ramblers, and so it should be. It was first introduced in 1882 by William Paul, a breeder and authority of the time responsible for a number of roses that are still very popular today. Its small pompon-like flowers of soft powdery pink are produced in large bunches amid large drooping leaves. It is a very vigorous rose and sends out fishing-rod-like growths on which it produces flowers the following season.

Paul, UK, late 19th century, summer flowering, 6 x 3.8 m (20 x 12 ft)

'Narrow Water'

A less vigorous rose and worth inclusion as it is an excellent all-round grower with lovely flowers and a capability of producing more than one flush in each season, often well into the autumn. The blooms are semi-double, soft pink in clusters and scented. Dark leaves provide a perfect background to them. Can be grown as a shrub.

Daisy Hill Nurseries, Ireland, about 1883, repeat flowering, 2.5 x 1.8 m (8 x 6 ft)

'Princess of Nassau'

A little-known variety but a favourite of mine in that its flower colouring, being chiefly white, is tinged with an ochre yellow. Semi-double and sporting a coronet of dusty orange anthers, the flowers are most attractive. This variety flowers in the summer and then again during the autumn, a very useful quality. It was rediscovered by the eminent rosarian Graham Thomas, who supplied my father with budwood to enable its reintroduction in 1982, although it is considerably older than this would suggest.

Of unknown origin, probably early 19th century, repeat flowering, 3 x 2.5 m (10 x 8 ft)

'The Garland'

I include this one not only because it is an excellent rose but also because of sentimental reasons. I spent a large part of my childhood living in an old farmhouse, where a specimen of 'The Garland' grew close to my bedroom window and each year I would enjoy its delicious perfume as it wafted into the house. I am taken back to this room every time I smell this rose. Flowers are semi-double, white tinged pink and appear in great profusion in midsummer. Leaves are mid- to dark green and there is an ample covering of vicious hooked thorns.

Wills, UK, 1835, summer flowering, 4.5 x 3 m (15 x 10 ft)

Multiflora ramblers

The direct descendants of *Rosa multiflora* are the most easy to identify but there are very many more fused with other groups. Among the ranks of these ramblers are some of the best known and most stunning ramblers available, many with the vigour to navigate their way through the branches of tall trees, over garden buildings and large pergolas, to the top and along large expanses of wall.

'Bobbie James'

This is a beautiful rambler with semi-double, slightly cupped pure white flowers borne in clusters against large fresh green leaves. It was introduced in 1961 and, compared to many others of its nature, has come to equal and in some cases surpass them. It is strong in growth with well-armed branches and is capable of scrambling naturally through a hedge. It is tolerant of poor soils and shade and will cope on a cool shady wall.

Sunningdale Nurseries, UK, 1961, summer flowering, 9 x 6 m (30 x 20 ft)

Below: 'Bobbie James' can reach a height of 10m (30ft).

'Francis E. Lester'

Another beautiful multiflora with individual flowers that are more dainty and, dare I say, more feminine than those of 'Bobbie James'. They are single, slightly cupped, white with pink around the edges of the petals and are perfumed. Small rounded hips follow in autumn. Leaves are dark, slim and elegant. It is a very popular garden rose.

Lester Rose Gardens, USA, 1946, summer flowering, 4.5 x 3 m (15 x 10 ft)

'Ghislaine de Féligonde'

One of the few ramblers that break the once-flowering pattern, this variety will produce a good second flush and will still be flowering in early autumn. It is most attractive and a little different in growth habit to the majority of the Multifloras; it is certainly less vigorous than many and produces dense rather than tall coverage. Flowers, in clusters, are fully double, open in a shade of apricot orange, sometimes tinged pink, and pale with age to a soft shade of buff.

Turbat, France, 1916, repeat flowering, 2.5 x 2.5 m (8 x 8 ft)

'Rambling Rector'

This is a very old and well-known cultivar, sometimes called 'Shakespeare's Musk'. Flowers are small, semi-double creamy white, fading to pure white with age and appear in large clusters, pervading the air with their fragrance. Growth is extremely vigorous and I am fond of seeing this variety growing through the branches of a tree, where the nodding clusters of flowers are well displayed against the greenery of the leaves. Clusters of hips replace the flowers later in the year.

Of unknown origin, very old, summer flowering, 6.x 4.5 m (20 x 15 ft)

Left: 'Rambling Rector', also often called 'Shakespeare's Musk', is ideal climbing through the branches of trees.

Above: 'Ghislaine de Féligonde' is a smaller rambler that produces flowers for most of the summer.

'Veilchenblau'

There are a few ramblers available in shades of lilac and purple and this is one of them. Semi-double flowers are violet purple, flecked white and fading to a grey shade of lilac with maturity. It is vigorous and strong growing and a good companion to the softer-shaded varieties.

Schmidt, Germany, 1909, summer flowering, 6.x 4.5 m (20 x 15 ft)

Sempervirens hybrids

In the Victorian era, these roses were referred to as the Evergreen roses and this is true for they retain their foliage in all but the most severe of winters. They are a dense-growing and, on the whole, vigorous group with pompon-style flowers.

'Adélaide d'Orléans'

Soft pink and gently fragrant small blooms are borne in clusters, *en masse* in midsummer. Foliage is dense on a plant with reasonable vigour. This French rose will tolerate poor soils and shade, useful through tree branches.

Jacques, France, 1826, summer flowering, 4.5 x 3 m (15 x 10 ft)

'Félicité Perpétue'

From clusters of small but plump buds emerge tight pompon flowers of creamy white with pink edging that are softly scented. Leaves are glossy and dark and will remain on the plant until the nastiest of frosts forces them to fall; stems are not overly endowed with thorns. A good, vigorous if not overwhelming rambler of beauty. There is a dwarf form of this rose, 'White Pet', that rarely exceeds a metre in height but will bloom well into the autumn.

Jacques, France, 1827, summer flowering, 4.5 x 3 m (15 x 10 ft)

'Spectabilis'

Creamy white flowers are tinged with lilac and nod in large clusters from an unassuming plant with dark green, semi-evergreen foliage. This is an old and reliable variety, tolerant of all but the

Below: 'Kiftsgate' is extremely fast growing.

most severe conditions. It is a good all-rounder which may occasionally produce a bloom or two after its first flush.

Of unknown origin, about 1850, summer flowering, 3 x 1.8 m (10 x 6 ft)

Other classified ramblers

The three varieties included here do not belong to any of the larger groups that appear in this section but to other, smaller classifications that I have not included. However, I did not wish to leave these three varieties out as they are important roses. Their classification is noted after the name.

'Kiftsgate' (*filipes*)

One of the best known 'tree climbers' with magnificent climbing capability. The single, scented cream to white flowers are borne in huge trusses and are followed by many small hips in the autumn. Growth is extremely vigorous with large bright green foliage and copper-nted young shoots. It will tolerate cool, dark aspects, shade and poor soil.

Murrell, UK, 1954, summer flowering, 9 x 6 m (30 x 20 ft)

'Mermaid' (*bracteata*)

The wonderful flowers of this rose are large, with wing-like petals, bright lemon yellow with pronounced stamens and a gentle fragrance. The almost evergreen foliage is large, rich green and glossy on slender growth that is well armed with nasty hooked thorns. It tolerates shade, but does not like frost and will die back in bad winters.

W. Paul, UK, 1917, continuous flowering, 9 x 6 m (30 x 20 ft)

'Sir Cedric Morris' (*glauca*)

This was one of a number of *Rosa glauca* seedlings found growing in the garden of the late Sir Frederick Ashton and it makes a staggering sight. Blooms are small and single

in huge trusses with small orange-red hips following later but it is the foliage I love best. It is soft grey, large and drooping in habit, a beautiful background to the flowers but also a feature in its own right. This is a very vigorous rose, ideal for growing through the branches of

Above: 'Sir Cedric Morris' has large, soft grey leaves and is very vigorous.

trees, and it will cope with the usual dryness at the roots there.

Beales, UK, 1979, summer flowering, 9 x 6 m (30 x 20 ft)

Species ramblers

While the majority of species roses are the forerunners of one or another race, or indeed several races of roses, they are also distinct in that they are the pure roses of nature. They are the only roses to grow true to type from seed, although there are some with slightly differing clones. They are an important group of roses that we should very much respect. Although some consider species roses to be boring, these people should look at them a little harder. Most are exquisite in their simple beauty and most, in fact nearly all, are far less prone to the effects of disease than hybrid roses.

Rosa arvensis

Also known as the Field Rose, *Rosa arvensis* is a native of Britain (in fact our only native with climbing capabilities) and Europe and can be found creeping through wild hedgerows, especially in southern England, hence its other name. It is strikingly beautiful with pure white single flowers bearing a ring of bright golden anthers, set off by dark foliage and dark pliable stems. It is worth growing as a garden rose if you have the space and will give a lovely display of hips in the autumn.

Europe, summer flowering, 6 x 3 m (20 x 10 ft)

Above: *Rosa arvensis* is extremely hardy.

Rosa helenae

I choose to include *Rosa helenae* as, in my opinion, it is one of the most beautiful, dainty-flowered species ramblers. It was originally was found growing wild in China by E.H. Wilson who named it after his wife. A vigorous rose, it produces large corymbs of single white blooms that are followed by glorious, small red hips in the autumn.

Wilson, China, 1907, summer flowering, 6.x 4.5 m (20 x 15 ft)

Rosa moschata

This is a very ancient rose, although there is no positive evidence of its original homeland, possibly Southern China or India. It is important in the family tree of roses for it has many descendants, both direct and indirect. Unlike *Rosa helenae,* it does not reach huge proportions and is a little later flowering than many, usually producing its blooms in mid- to late summer. Flowers are creamy white, single in form and flat, held in large clusters. Probably due to its later flowering period it does not always set hips.

16th century, summer flowering, 2.5 x 1.8 m (8 x 6 ft)

Rosa mulliganii

I include this in my limited choice of species rambling roses not because it is hugely important in the history of roses, but because it deserves space in the garden today. Small white flowers are single, held in clusters and exude a wonderful delicate fragrance with a banana-like aroma. Leaves are grey green, tinted purple when young. A fairly vigorous rose, which was often, until recently, misnamed *Rosa longicuspis*.

China, 1917, summer flowering, 4.5 x 3 m (15 x 10 ft)

Rosa multiflora

Until recently this variety was often used as an understock and it is a strong-growing hardy species. Like *Rosa moschata*, it has many important descendants, most of which are also hardy and strong growing. When mature it will produce small, creamy white blooms in huge abundance followed by orange red oval fruits. This is a rose tolerant of most poor growing situations.

Asia, 12th century, summer flowering, 4.5 x 3 m (15 x 10 ft)

Rosa wichuraiana

Discovered in China in 1860 by the German plant collector Max Ernst Wichura, this is an interesting rose that is responsible for many offspring. Flowers in clusters are neat and white followed by small orange vermilion hips in the autumn. One particular trait, well demonstrated in many of the hybrid wichuraianas, is its extremely glossy dark foliage. I include it in this section as it is difficult to place elsewhere given the breakdown I have elected to use. It could also be listed as a procumbent or climbing rose (it is as well suited to sprawling over banks and through hedges), and many of its direct offspring are regularly listed in both categories. This is a useful rambling rose.

Wilson, 1860, summer flowering, 1.8 x 6 m (6 x 20 ft)

Wichuraiana hybrids

While *Rosa wichuraiana* is, in essence, a rambler with diverse uses (good on a wall, scrambling through hedges and over banks or into trees), its offspring could easily be split in two groups, some falling into the rambling category and fewer others with more of a climbing tendency. This is due largely to interbreeding, some resulting hybrids tending to scramble and produce just one flush of flowers each year, the others being less rampant and, in a few cases, repeat flowering. Whichever tendency they display, this is an excellent group of roses with few having a weakness to disease, although those that do are true martyrs.

'Albéric Barbier'

This is one of the best ramblers available in terms of health and freedom of flower and one of the most successful at remaining evergreen. Foliage is dark and glossy, an ideal foil for shapely white-tinged lemon flowers. Growth is pliable and easily trained. Although technically summer flowering, a mature plant will give the occasional repeat bloom.

Barbier, France, 1900, summer flowering, 4.5 x 3 m (15 x 10 ft)

'Albertine'

This is one of the best known and best loved roses of all and, although truly charming, it is also sadly one of the least resistant to disease. Having said this, its susceptibility to mildew and, in my experience, rust can be controlled with sprays provided they are employed before disease strikes, which is not usually until after the flowers have passed. Albertine has beautiful, blowsy, salmon pink flowers that fade with age to near blush. They are very heavily scented. It has gorgeous plum-coloured young shoots and leaves and is relatively vigorous.

Barbier, France, 1921, summer flowering, 4.5 x 3 m (15 x 10 ft)

'Dorothy Perkins'

This is another famous old variety found in many gardens. Flowers are small, clear pink, scented and are borne in bunches on arching branches. Leaves are small and glossy but sadly rather prone to mildew after flowering. There are several similar varieties available such as crimson 'Excelsa' and the deeper pink 'Minnehaha', all of which are commonly available as weeping standards.

Jackson and Perkins, USA, 1902, summer flowering, 3 x 2.5 m (10 x 8 ft)

'Ethel'

I include 'Ethel' as a very useful rose. Its climbing capabilities are to be marvelled at as it can reach great heights in a short time in comparison to other roses. Flowers are small and cupped but are produced in large trusses against glossy leaves and well-armed branches. It is a seedling of 'Dorothy Perkins' but does not share its readiness to fall prey to disease. Some nurseries list a variety by the name of 'Belvedere' and it is possible that they are one and the same rose.

Turner, UK, 1912, summer flowering, 6.x 4.5 m (20 x 15 ft)

'Evangeline'

Semi-double blooms are creamy white flushed pink at the petal edges, and are borne in large trusses a little later in the summer than those of many ramblers. Leaves are large and leathery and borne on a strong growing, relatively vigorous plant.

Walsh, USA, 1906, summer flowering, 6.x 4.5 m (20 x 15 ft)

'Gardenia'

This has to be one of my all-time favourite roses. Individually, the flowers are not large or stunning, but when in full flush they almost obliterate the dark glossy foliage and fill the air with a fruity aroma. Their colouring is best described as cream to buff, fading slightly with age, and they are slightly ragged with many smallish petals.

Manda, USA, 1899, summer flowering, 6.x 4.5 m (20 x 15 ft)

'New Dawn'

This is probably the most 'all-round' well-tested climber you will find. There are others that share its generosity of flower, health and perfume, but they have been around for a shorter time and are less well known. It is a sport of the rose 'Dr Van Fleet', introduced in the USA in 1930, to which it is identical in all respects but remontancy of flower. Buds are plump and open to reveal soft pink, semi-double, pointed and perfumed blooms that become almost flat before falling. Leaves are dark and glossy and stems bear average quantities of thorns. Growth is not hugely vigorous but ample enough to cover most supports with ease. This is an outstanding rose in all respects, except that because it does all that is asked of a rose by every gardener every where, it lacks that the quality of being outstanding in any one respect. If you have a smaller garden and need a bit of everything in a climber then this is the rose to go for.

Somerset Rose Co., USA, 1930, continuous flowering, 3 x 2.5 m (10 x 8 ft)

'Sanders White'

Dark glossy foliage and pliable growth are just two of the merits of this rambler. Flowers are small in nodding clusters with the occasional solitary bloom, white and double. It is a healthy variety of medium vigour that will give good coverage whether grown against a wall or on a pillar.

Sanders and Sons, UK, 1912, summer flowering, 3.8 x 2.5 m (12 x 8ft)

Right: The dark leaves of 'Gardenia' are a contrasting foil for the fruity scented flowers.

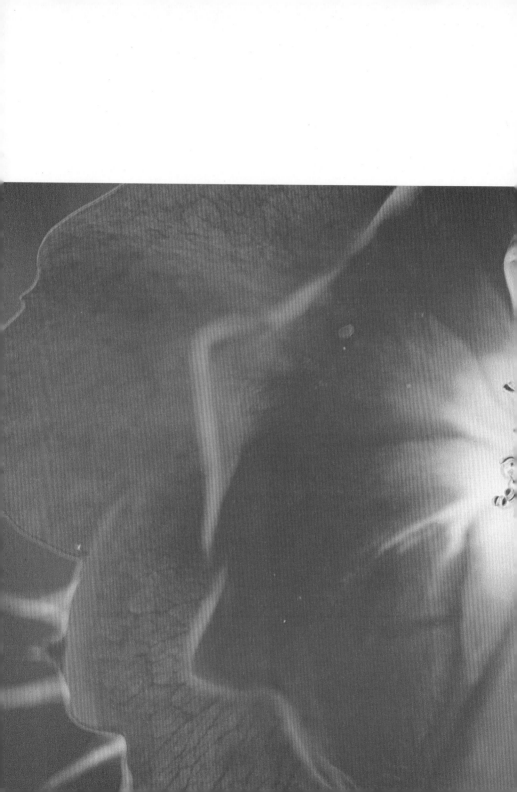

Further information

Recommended roses for specific situations

When considering the roses to include in a garden you may have specific needs, such as perfume or difficult sites, that require thought. The following lists may be of help, although due to limited space they are in no way comprehensive. All these roses are described in the Plant Directory.

For shaded places

Roses prefer to have some light available to them, but can thrive in dappled shade or a place that is shaded for part of the day. If there is a shaded place in the garden that would benefit from the inclusion of a rose, the following are good candidates.

Shrub and Bush roses
'Alba Semiplena'
'Buff Beauty'
'Mme Isaac Pereire'
'Regensberg'
'Westerland'

Climbers and ramblers
'City of York'
'Félicité Perpétue'
'Gardenia'
'Golden Showers'
'Souvenir du Docteur Jamain'

Climbers and ramblers for north-facing walls

In all but the severest of winters, when they may suffer some die back, the following roses will cope with a wall in full shade.

'Blush Noisette'
'Ghislaine de Féligonde'
'Iceberg, Climbing'
'Mme Alfred Carrière'
'New Dawn'

For poor soils

Not all roses will tolerate very poor soil but there are a few that cope quite well. Do everything possible to improve the soil before planting, however.

Shrub and Bush roses
'Belle Poitevine'
'Celestial'
'Comte de Chambord'
'Fantin Latour'
'Margaret Merril'

Climbers and ramblers
'Albéric Barbier'
'Leverkusen'
'Mme Caroline Testout'
'Paul's Himalayan Musk'
'Veilchenblau'

For ornamental hips

Roses should be considered for providing colour other than that of their flowers. The following varieties set good hips and in some cases will show autumn colour in their foliage as well. Although some modern Bush roses will produce hips, the majority will have been removed during the process of dead-heading. Therefore they are not the best candidates if a stunning display is desired.

Shrub roses
'Mary Queen of Scots'
'Lord Penzance'
Rosa glauca
Rosa virginiana
'Scabrosa'

Climbers and ramblers
'Kiftsgate'
'Mme Grégoire Staechelin'

Further information

'Rambling Rector'
Rosa helenae
Rosa mulliganii

Shrub Roses for hedging

While a couple of the roses mentioned below are Rugosas, it is fair to say that nearly all of that group are good hedging plants. Those listed below are all dense and tidy in growth, ideal for a formal hedge.

'Blanc Double de Coubert'
'Roseraie de l'Hay'
'Queen Elizabeth'
'Felicia'
'Maiden's Blush Great'

Short- to medium-growing pillar roses

Not all climbers are good candidates for a pillar. Those that grow best in such a situation are of less vigour with upright growth.

'Aloha'
'Dublin Bay'
'Eden Rose 88'
'Golden Showers'
'Kathleen Harrop'

Vigorous ramblers for climbing through trees

If you wish to grow a rose through the branches of a tree or over a tumbledown eyesore, it will need great prowess as a climber. Those below are ideal.

'Ethel'
'Kiftsgate'
'Rambling Rector'
Rosa mulliganii
'Sir Cedric Morris'

For flowers over a long period

While once-flowering roses usually provide the most stunning displays, there are roses that will flower well into the autumn.

Shrub and Bush roses
'Bonica 82'
'Felicia'
'Jacqueline du Pré'
'Macmillan Nurse'
'Norwich Castle'

Climbers and ramblers
'Aloha'
'Dublin Bay'
'Gloire de Dijon'
'Mme Alfred Carrière'
'New Dawn'

For perfume

For some people, a rose must be perfumed to have garden value but not all roses are. The following are all well scented, in my opinion, but this is a controversial issue. The scent of a particular variety may appeal to many, but to others it may seem devoid of any perfume.

Shrub and Bush roses
'Anna Pavlova'
'Comte de Chambord'
'Ferdinand Pichard'
'Kazanlik'
'Mme Isaac Pereire'

Climbers and ramblers
'Aloha'
'Blairi Number Two'
'Gardenia'
'Gloire de Dijon'
'Sombreuil'

For smaller gardens

Not everyone has the space for large shrub roses or towering climbers. Those listed below are compact in habit and should not outgrow their welcome. The climbers and ramblers are easily controlled. All these roses are also candidates for growing in containers.

Shrub and Bush roses

'Alfred de Dalmas'
'Comte de Chambord'
'Rose de Meaux'
'Sweet Dream'
'Twenty-fifth'

Climbers and ramblers

'Aloha'
'Blush Noisette'
'Ghislaine de Féligonde'
'Narrow Water'
'Zéphirine Drouhin'

For wild gardens and woodland

When planting roses in such situations it is best to choose those that will not only complement the area but which will also cope well if not tended to regularly. Ramblers work well through the branches of trees or if just left to tumble over the ground.

Shrub roses

'Common Moss'
'Grouse'
Rosa canina
Rosa glauca
Rosa virginiana

Ramblers

'Kiftsgate'
'Rambling Rector'
Rosa arvensis
Rosa helenae
Rosa wichuraiana

Rose societies

Both the American and British Rose Societies are large bodies with membership advantages. They produce regular publications and offer advice to members should they need it.

UNITED KINGDOM
THE ROYAL NATIONAL ROSE SOCIETY
Chiswell Green Lane, St Albans, Hertfordshire, AL2 3NR
www.rnrs.org

USA
THE AMERICAN ROSE SOCIETY
PO Box 30,000, Shreveport, Louisiana, 71130
www.ars.org

HERITAGE ROSE FOUNDATION
PO Box 831414, Richardson, TX 75083
www.heritagerosefoundation.org

Bibliography

Beales, Amanda, Old Fashioned Roses, Cassell, 1990
Beales, Amanda, Rose Basics, Hamlyn, 1999
Beales, Peter, Classic Roses, revised edition, Collins Harvill, 1997
Beales, Peter, Roses, HarperCollins, 1992
Beales, Peter, Twentieth Century Roses, Collins Harvill, 1988
Jekyll, Gertrude and Mawley, Edward, Roses for English Gardens, Antique Collectors Club, reprinted 1990
Le Rougetel, Hazel, A Heritage of Roses, Unwin Hyman, 1988
Paterson, Allen, The History of the Rose, Collins, 1983
Royal National Rose Society, How to Grow Roses, 1992
Scanniello, Stephen and Bayard, Tania, Roses of America, Henry Holt, 1990
Thomas, Graham Stuart, The Old Shrub Roses, Dent, 1986
Various authors, Botanica's Roses (The Encyclopedia Of Roses), Grange Books, 1998

Glossary

Acid A state of the soil where the pH is less than 7.

Alkaline A state of the soil where the pH is more than 7.

Anther The part of the stamen containing pollen.

Bare-rooted The term describing roses dug up and sold without being potted.

Bud The unopened flower.

Budding A form of propagation involving the placing of a scion into a rootstock.

Calyx The green leaves protecting the flower in bud.

Cambium A layer of growth cells immediately below the bark.

Chlorosis The discolouring of leaves associated with deficiencies.

Cluster A group of flowers together growing from one stem.

Continuous flowering Flowers appear successively throughout the season.

Division A form of propagation involving the transplanting of suckers.

Emasculation The removal of all male parts of the flower during hybridization.

Fertilization The fusion of the male pollen with the ovule of the female parent.

Fibrous root The hairy parts of rose roots, with most growth activity.

Germination The term used to describe the appearance of a seedling from a fertilized seed.

Glaucous A grey to blue colouring.

Grafting A method of propagation where material from one rose is encouraged to bond with the roots of another.

Heel The small piece of two-year-old bark found at the base of heel cuttings.

Heeling-in A method of storing bare-rooted roses in the ground before planting.

Hip The seed-carrying fruit of roses.

Hybrid A variety derived from two other roses.

Hybridization The creation of new rose varieties.

Lax An open, loose habit of growth.

Layering A method of propagation involving burying a section of a branch while still growing so that roots develop.

Moss The hairy down found on some roses.

Mulch An application of usually organic material spread over the ground.

Node The place at a leaf joint where a bud is to be found.

Nutrient A water-soluble beneficial substance found in the soil and taken up by the roots.

Pegging-down A way of training shrub roses so that they are broad in growth.

pH The scale on which alkalinity and acidity are measured in the soil.

Pollinate The application of male pollen to the female stigma of a separate flower during the process of hybridization.

Procumbent A manner of growth being broader than tall.

Pruning The cutting back of plants to encourage young growth and improved flowering.

Receptacle The swollen area found at the base of the flower, which will later become the hip.

Reflexed A flower form where the petals furl back on the open flower.

Repeat flowering Flowers appear in definite waves during the season.

Rootstock The rose used for the host roots on budded and grafted plants.

Scion The piece of plant stem used in budding and grafting which will become the branches of the plant, attached to the rootstock.

Seedling An unnamed variety of rose, often awaiting introduction.

Spine A long, narrow, sharp thorn.

Spore The seed of fungal diseases.

Sport A variety which has come about as a mutation on another rose.

Stamen Stamens make up the whorl, which surrounds the stigma within a flower.

Stigma The very centre of the rose with receptive cells prepared to accept pollen.

Suckers The branches that grow from roots separate from the main plant.

Summer flowering Flowering just once during the summer.

Tap root The main and thickest roots of the root system.

Union The place on a budded or grafted plant where branches and roots join.

Index

Acknowledgements

I aim to keep this short and mention only a few people by name. All others will hopefully realise how grateful I have been for their support whilst writing this book.

However, I would like to convey feelings of gratitude to a few. To my Editor, Karen O'Grady, for her patience and dedication and Mark Winwood, for portraying in pictures the ambience of the rose, a magic that is difficult to put into words. I thank my entire family circle and fellow staff for all they have done but in particular I owe my father and mentor, Peter Beales, very much for teaching me what I know and my Mother and brother for their encouragement. Lastly to the people I dedicate this book to, those who continually put up with so much so that I may pursue my love of roses, my husband David and children Laura and Alexander.

Executive Editor: Sarah Ford
Editor: Kate Tuckett
Executive Art Editor: Geoff Fennell
Designer: Janis Utton
Assistant Production Controller: Nosheen Shan

Photographic Acknowledgements

Acknowledgements in Source Order

Peter Beales 9, 73
Garden Picture Library 35; /Howard Rice 6–7, 10–11
Octopus Publishing Group Limited/Sean Myers 23 top left, 23 bottom left, 24 top right, 25 top right, 25 bottom left, 26, 28–29, 32 top left, 32 bottom left, 33 top, 33 centre, 33 bottom, 36 bottom left, 39 top, 39 bottom, 40, 42, 43 top right, 44–45, 49, 50 top centre, 50 top left, 64; /Mark Winwood 1, 2–3, 4–5, 12 top right, 12 bottom left, 13, 14, 15 top left, 15 bottom right, 16, 17, 18–19, 20 top right, 20 bottom left, 21, 22 top left, 22 top right, 22 bottom right, 23 top right, 27, 30 top, 30 centre, 30 bottom, 34, 36 top right, 37 top right, 37 bottom left, 41, 43 bottom left, 46 top left, 46 top right, 46 bottom left, 46 bottom right, 46 bottom centre left, 46 bottom centre right, 46 top centre right, 46 top centre left, 46–47 bottom, 47 bottom right, 47 bottom centre, 51 top left, 51 bottom right, 52 top left, 52 top right, 53 top left, 53 top right, 54 top left, 54 top right, 55 top centre, 55 top left, 55 centre left, 55 top right, 57, 58–59, 60, 61, 62 top right, 62 bottom, 63, 65, 66, 67 top left, 67 bottom right, 68–69, 71, 72, 74, 75, 77, 79, 80, 81, 82, 84, 85, 86 top right, 86 bottom left, 87, 88, 89, 90, 91, 92, 93, 94, 95, 96, 97, 98, 99 top left, 99 bottom right, 101, 102, 103, 104, 105, 106, 107 top right, 107 bottom left, 109, 110 top right, 110 bottom left, 111, 112, 113, 114, 115, 116, 119, 120–121